FINE FURNITURE for a lifetime

GLEN HUEY

POPULAR WOODWORKING BOOKS
CINCINNATI, OHIO
www.popularwoodworking.com

READ THIS IMPORTANT SAFETY NOTICE

To prevent accidents, keep safety in mind while you work. Use the safety guards installed on power equipment; they are for your protection. When working on power equipment, keep fingers away from saw blades, wear safety goggles to prevent injuries from flying wood chips and sawdust, wear headphones to protect your hearing, and consider installing a dust vacuum to reduce the amount of airborne sawdust in your woodshop. Don't wear loose clothing, such as neckties or shirts with loose sleeves, or jewelry, such as rings, necklaces or bracelets, when working on power equipment. Tie back long hair to prevent it from getting caught in your equipment. People who are sensitive to certain chemicals should check the chemical content of any product before using it. The authors and editors who compiled this book have tried to make the contents as accurate and correct as possible. Plans, illustrations, photographs and text have been carefully checked. All instructions, plans and projects should be carefully read, studied and understood before beginning construction. Due to the variability of local conditions, construction materials, skill levels, etc., neither the author nor Popular Woodworking Books assumes any responsibility for any accidents, injuries, damages or other losses incurred resulting from the material presented in this book. Prices listed for supplies and equipment were current at the time of publication and are subject to change.

METRIC CONVERSION CHART

TO CONVERT	TO	MULTIPLY BY
Inches	Centimeters	2.54
Centimeters	Inches	0.4
Feet	Centimeters	30.5
Centimeters	Feet	0.03
Yards	Meters	0.9
Meters	Yards	1.1
Sq. Inches	Sq. Centimeters	6.45
Sq. Centimeters	Sq. Inches	0.16
Sq. Feet	Sq. Meters	0.09
Sq. Meters	Sq. Feet	10.8
Sq. Yards	Sq. Meters	0.8
Sq. Meters	Sq. Yards	1.2
Pounds	Kilograms	0.45
Kilograms	Pounds	2.2
Ounces	Grams	28.4
Grams	Ounces	0.04

Fine Furniture for a Lifetime: includes 10 elegant projects. Copyright © 2002 by Glen Huey. Manufactured in Singapore. All rights reserved. No part of this book may be reproduced in any form or by any electronic or mechanical means, including information storage and retrieval systems, without permission in writing from the publisher, except by a reviewer, who may quote brief passages in a review. Published by Popular Woodworking Books, an imprint of F&W Publications, Inc., 4700 East Galbraith Road, Cincinnati, Ohio, 45236. (800) 289-0963. First edition.

Visit our Web site at www.popularwoodworking.com for more information and resources for woodworkers.

Other fine Popular Woodworking Books are available from your local bookstore or direct from the publisher.

07   06   05   04   03   6   5   4   3   2

Library of Congress Cataloging-in-Publication Data

Huey, Glen
    Fine furniture for a lifetime : includes 10 elegant projects / by Glen Huey.
      p. cm.
    Includes index.
    ISBN 1-55870-593-7
    1. Furniture making--Amateurs' manuals. 2. Furniture--United States--Reproduction--Amateurs' manuals. I. Title.

TT195 .H84 2002
684.1--dc21
                                    2001051145

Edited by Jennifer Churchill
Designed by Brian Roeth
Interior layout by Kathy Gardner
Lead photography by Al Parrish
Step-by-step photography by Glen Huey
Production coordinated by Sara Dumford
Technical illustrations by Len Churchill
Editorial assistance by Megan Williamson
Acquisitions editor: Jim Stack

RESOURCES

Horton Brasses, Inc.
Hardware
P.O. Box 95
Cromwell, CT 06416
(800) 754-9127
www.horton-brasses.com

Bendheim's
Restoration Glass
61 Willett Street
Passaic, NJ 07055
(800) 835-5304
www.bendheim.com

Donald Durham Company
Durham's Rock Hard Water Putty
Box 804-E
Des Moines, IA 50304
www.waterputty.com

Woodcraft Supply Corp.
Hardware
1177 Rosemar Road
Parkersburg, WV 26101
www.woodcraft.com

Timbered Ridge
Bed Canopies, Appalachian Folk Art
315 E. Glade St.
Glade Spring, VA 24340
276-429-3600

about the author

Glen Huey was born and raised in Ohio. The middle child of three boys, he decided at the age of 14 to use his father's tools (and his father's help) to build a Sheraton field bed, which he has to this day.

Upon his graduation from the University of Cincinnati, Glen began building homes. After a couple of career changes and a yearning to expand his woodworking, he opened a company focused on designing and building projects for homebuilders in the area.

After completing a major project, and with a gentle push from his wife (who tired of hearing him lament about wanting to build furniture), he changed the focus of his work and began to create 18th- and 19th-century period designs.

Today he is a contributing editor to *Popular Woodworking* magazine and travels to exhibit at shows across the country. Glen's pieces have been featured in several national magazines. He lives with his wife, Laurie, and continues to work with his father at Malcolm L. Huey & Son in Middletown, Ohio.

acknowledgements

Many thanks:

To Jim Stack and Jennifer Churchill of Popular Woodworking Books. Jim gave me the opportunity, and both Jim and Jennifer guided me through the process of putting this book together.

To the editors of *Popular Woodworking* magazine. They have exposed me to a different area of the woodworking business and I thank them for choosing me to join in their efforts.

To Al Parrish for photography that makes these projects look their best. Without his vast knowledge and assistance, I may still be trying to figure out how to get the overabundance of green out of my shop photographs.

To Jay Cobb, whom I have known for the better part of my life and who has graciously opened his home and antique collection to me whenever I have asked.

And to Eileen Roberts, Richard and Elizabeth Williams, Edward Brown and my other customers for allowing me to continue creating furniture.

dedication

To my wife, Laurie. She is inspiring and enthusiastic about my work, has assumed many new responsibilities and tasks to allow me to continue my passion, and knows how and when to push me a bit further. It is because of her that I returned to what I knew I was supposed to do.

To my parents, Malcolm and Doris: I followed my father into many careers and he taught me anything that I was willing to learn. He and my mother provided the tools, both for woodworking and for life, that I needed to become who I am.

table of
CONTENTS

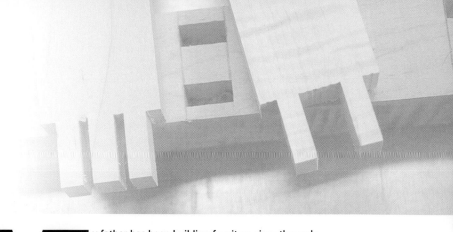

introduction

My father has been building furniture since the early 1970s. During that time, with a full selection of tools easily accessible to me, I became interested in building furniture. At the age of 14, with great help from Dad, I built my first piece — a Sheraton bed that I still have to this day. Some years later I decided to pursue my passion — the building of 18th- and 19th-century reproduction furniture.

Why 18th and 19th century? First, and most importantly, this is the era and style that I most admire. The best designs were created during this period in American history. The development of Queen Anne, Chippendale and Federal styles provided masterpieces for city patrons and consequently the pieces that were copied by the rural craftsman. Add to this the Shaker movement with its distinct style, and who could ask for better craftsmanship to copy? These are proven designs that are timeless.

Also, in my opinion, this era presented the best furniture-making skills. The use of handcrafted techniques such as mortise-and-tenon joinery and dovetailed drawers along with the great hardwoods result in a piece in which one can be proud. I believe that a handcrafted piece of furniture carries with it a bit of its maker's soul into the future.

The collection described in this book exhibits all periods in our history, pieces built by the finest city and rural craftsmen of their time, as well as furniture built by the Shakers with their simplistic designs. ∎

construction TECHNIQUES

ogee-bracket feet

AS YOU EXAMINE THE PROJECTS throughout this book, you will find that there are a number of similarities that arise. Here are some simple techniques that I enjoy using and some methods of work I feel will help you to present a piece of furniture in the best manner possible and will exhibit quality workmanship.

Let's start at the bottom: First, we have the ogee-bracket feet shown in the Chippendale Entertainment Center and the Chester County Tall Chest. The steps shown here will result in a great foot, and they are the basic steps for making straight-bracket feet, as well.

Next, and most important, is the drawer construction. My philosophy is simple: dovetails. There is no better joint to use and no better method that reveals quality of construction. And there is no better dovetail than the hand-cut type. Of the 10 projects presented here, all but two use hand-cut dovetails. Follow these steps and you will be pleased with the results while building confidence in your ability.

Next, I have developed a trait of connecting my tops and frames with wooden clips. The slot is created in the case or table aprons with a standard biscuit joiner set for a No. 20 biscuit. By cutting the biscuit slot rather than a lengthy groove, you will not weaken the piece.

Draw the ogee foot design on the end of your stock and set the blade height. Set the temporary fence so that the blade enters and exits the stock in line with the design, and make multiple passes over the blade, removing the waste.

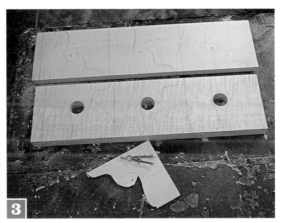

Using a pattern, lay out the feet, making sure that you have the pieces for three pairs. Drill the appropriate hole size, and cut the foot profile.

Use the saw to trim as close to the design as possible, then remove any additional waste with a plane or scraper. Rough sand to a finished profile.

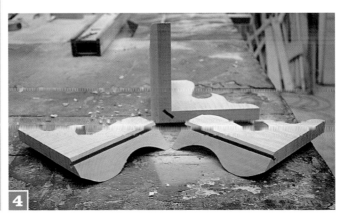

Cut for a spline in each pair of feet as shown, and assemble.

drawer basics: hand-cut dovetails

1

After cutting the drawer fronts to plan, run the four edges with a $^3/_{16}$" roundover bit set to $^1/_4$" depth.

2

Create a $^3/_8$" x $^1/_2$" rabbet along the ends and top of the drawer front, forming a lipped edge.

3

Lay out and cut the pins on the drawer sides, and remove the tail area waste.

4

Set the cut side onto the back, which is scribed to the side thickness and aligned at the top edge. Mark the back piece for the tail locations, cut on the inside of the pin area and remove the waste.

5

Lay out and cut the pins on the drawer fronts and remove the waste. (Notice the overcut saw lines; these indicate a hand-cut dovetailed drawer.) Set the drawer front on the sides. Align the top edges, and mark the tails onto the sides as shown. Remove the waste. Fit the pieces together.

6

Next, run a groove of $^5/_{16}$" x $^1/_4$" along each side and the front for the drawer bottom. Sand the interior of the drawer box pieces and glue the drawer box.

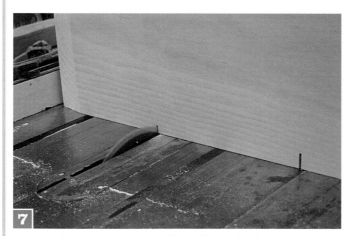

7

Next, cut the drawer bottoms to fit, and bevel the three edges to allow it to slide into the grooves in the drawer parts. The grain should run across the drawer. With the bottom in place, mark the inside edge on the bottom where it meets the drawer back. Place a saw cut to that height into the bottom.

8

Sand the exterior of the drawers, apply a dab of glue in two locations on the drawer front, and slide the sanded bottom into the drawer box. Nail through the saw cut in the bottom panel and into the drawer back. This secures the bottom and allows it to move with humidity changes.

wood clips

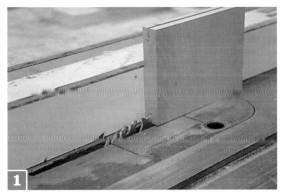

This setup works with a 1¹/₄" screw! Begin with a block of selected hardwood that is 4¹/₄" long and approximately 5" wide by ³/₄" thick. Set the fence at ¹/₄" and raise the blade height to ¹/₂". Run the piece over the blade, cutting the end grain. Cut both ends.

Reposition the height of the blade to ¹/₂" and set the fence to remove the waste portion, creating a ¹/₂" x ¹/₂" rabbet. Again, cut both ends.

Set the fence at ⁷/₈" and rip the block into pieces. In a slot created by a biscuit joiner, ⁷/₈" works best.

Using the miter gauge and a temporary fence, cut each ripped piece into two wooden clips.

Predrill and counterbore for a No. 8 x 1¹/₄" wood screw, then slide the clip into the slot created in your project and install the screw.

shaker
PRESS CUPBOARD

WHEN I FIRST DISCOVERED THIS CUPBOARD IN JOHN KASSAY'S *The Book of Shaker Furniture* (University of Massachusetts Press, 1980), it jumped from the pages and begged me to build it. The original version that I built featured a blind-door cupboard, but a friend at a furniture show suggested I build it with glass doors. I followed her advice and…what a difference!

This piece originated in the Pleasant Hill, Kentucky, Shaker community in the late 1800s. It's called a press cupboard because its flat, sturdy construction helped to press the linens stacked neatly inside. With the addition of the glass doors, this piece becomes a showplace for any treasured collection.

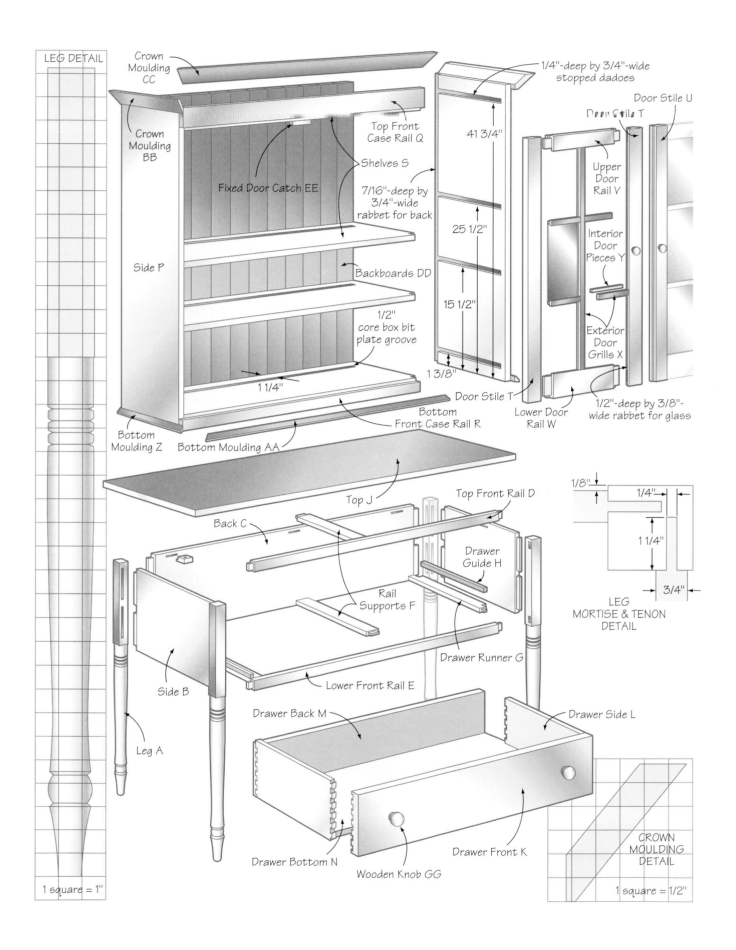

LEG DETAIL

Crown Moulding CC

Crown Moulding BB

Top Front Case Rail Q

Shelves S

Fixed Door Catch EE

7/16"-deep by 3/4"-wide rabbet for back

Side P

Backboards DD

1/2" core box bit plate groove

1 1/4"

Bottom Moulding Z

Bottom Moulding AA

Bottom Front Case Rail R

1/4"-deep by 3/4"-wide stopped dadoes

Door Stile U

Door Stile T

41 3/4"

Upper Door Rail V

Interior Door Pieces Y

25 1/2"

15 1/2"

Exterior Door Grills X

1 3/8"

Door Stile T

Lower Door Rail W

1/2"-deep by 3/8"-wide rabbet for glass

Top J

Top Front Rail D

Back C

Drawer Guide H

Rail Supports F

1/8"

1/4"

1 1/4"

3/4"

LEG MORTISE & TENON DETAIL

Drawer Runner G

Side B

Lower Front Rail E

Leg A

Drawer Back M

Drawer Side L

Drawer Bottom N

Wooden Knob GG

Drawer Front K

CROWN MOULDING DETAIL

1 square = 1/2"

1 square = 1"

cutting list | **inches**

SHAKER PRESS CUPBOARD

LOWER SECTION CASE PIECES

REFERENCE	QUANTITY	PART	STOCK	THICKNESS	WIDTH	LENGTH	COMMENTS
A	4	Legs	P	$1^1/_8$	$1^1/_8$	$34^1/_4$	
B	2	Sides	P	$3/_4$	11	$17^1/_4$	$1^1/_4$" TBE
C	1	Back	S	$3/_4$	11	$42^1/_4$	$1^1/_4$" TBE
D	1	Top Front Rail	P	$3/_4$	$1^1/_4$	$42^1/_4$	$1^1/_4$" TBE
E	1	Lower Front Rail	P	$3/_4$	$1^1/_4$	$42^1/_4$	$1^1/_4$" TBE
F	2	Rail Supports	S	$3/_4$	2	$18^1/_8$	$1/_2$" TBE
G	2	Drawer Runners	S	$3/_4$	$2^1/_8$	$17^3/_8$	$1/_2$" TOE
H	2	Drawer Guides	S	$1/_2$	$13/_{16}$	$14^5/_8$	
J	1	Top	P	$3/_4$	20	$47^1/_2$	
K	1	Drawer Front	P	$7/_8$	$8^3/_8$	$39^5/_8$	
L	2	Drawer Sides	S	$1/_2$	$8^1/_4$	$15^1/_2$	
M	1	Drawer Back	S	$1/_2$	$8^1/_4$	$39^5/_8$	
N	1	Drawer Bottom	S	$5/_8$	$15^1/_2$	39	

UPPER SECTION CASE PIECES

REFERENCE	QUANTITY	PART	STOCK	THICKNESS	WIDTH	LENGTH	COMMENTS
P	2	Sides	P	$3/_4$	12	45	
Q	1	Top Front Case Rail	P	$3/_4$	$5^1/_2$	39	
R	1	Bottom Front Case Rail	P	$3/_4$	$1^3/_4$	39	
S	4	Top, Bottom and Shelves	P	$3/_4$	$11^1/_4$	$37^3/_4$	
T	3	Door Stiles	P	$3/_4$	3	$37^1/_2$	
U	1	Door Stiles	P	$3/_4$	$3^1/_4$	$37^1/_2$	
V	2	Upper Door Rails	P	$3/_4$	$3^3/_4$	16	$1^1/_4$" TBE
W	2	Lower Door Rails	P	$3/_4$	$4^1/_2$	16	$1^1/_4$" TBE
X	4	Exterior Door Grills	P	$1/_4$	$3/_4$	30	
Y	4	Interior Door Pieces	P	$1/_4$	$1/_2$	30	
Z	2	Bottom Moulding	P	$5/_8$	$1^1/_2$	16	
AA	1	Bottom Moulding	P	$5/_8$	$1^1/_2$	42	
BB	2	Crown Moulding	P	$3/_4$	4	16	
CC	1	Crown Moulding	P	$3/_4$	4	42	
DD	1	Backboards	P	$5/_8$	$38^3/_8$	$42^1/_2$	made in many pieces
EE	1	Fixed Door Catch	S	$3/_4$	1	$3^1/_4$	
FF	2	Wooden Knobs	P			$1^1/_4$	
GG	2	Wooden Knobs	P			2	

P = Primary Wood

S = Secondary Wood

TBE = Tenon Both Ends

TOE = Tenon One End

hardware and supplies

Door hinges	2 prs., $2^1/_2$" in length
Slot-head wood screws	No. 8 x $1^1/_4$"
Clout or shingle nail for backboards	$1^1/_2$"
Fine finish nail for mouldings	$1^1/_2$"

cutting list | millimeters

SHAKER PRESS CUPBOARD

LOWER SECTION CASE PIECES

REFERENCE	QUANTITY	PART	STOCK	THICKNESS	WIDTH	LENGTH	COMMENTS
A	4	Legs	P	47	47	870	
B	2	Sides	P	19	279	438	32mm TBE
C	1	Back	S	19	279	1073	32mm TBE
D	1	Top Front Rail	P	19	32	1073	32mm TBE
E	1	Lower Front Rail	P	19	32	1073	32mm TBE
F	2	Rail Supports	S	19	51	460	13mm TBE
G	2	Drawer Runners	S	19	54	442	13mm TOE
H	2	Drawer Guides	S	13	30	372	
J	1	Top	P	19	508	1207	
K	1	Drawer Front	P	22	213	1007	
L	2	Drawer Sides	S	13	209	394	
M	1	Drawer Back	S	13	209	1007	
N	1	Drawer Bottom	S	16	394	991	

UPPER SECTION CASE PIECES

REFERENCE	QUANTITY	PART	STOCK	THICKNESS	WIDTH	LENGTH	COMMENTS
P	2	Sides	P	19	305	1143	
Q	1	Top Front Case Rail	P	19	140	991	
R	1	Bottom Front Case Rail	P	19	45	991	
S	4	Top, Bottom and Shelves	P	19	285	959	
T	3	Door Stiles	P	19	76	953	
U	1	Door Stiles	P	19	82	953	
V	2	Upper Door Rails	P	19	95	406	32mm TBE
W	2	Lower Door Rails	P	19	115	406	32mm TBE
X	4	Exterior Door Grills	P	6	19	762	
Y	4	Interior Door Pieces	P	6	13	762	
Z	2	Bottom Moulding	P	16	38	406	
AA	1	Bottom Moulding	P	16	38	1067	
BB	2	Crown Moulding	P	19	102	406	
CC	1	Crown Moulding	P	19	102	1067	
DD	1	Back	P	16	975	1080	made in many pieces
EE	1	Fixed Door Catch	S	19	25	82	
FF	2	Wooden Knobs	P			32	
GG	2	Wooden Knobs	P			51	

P = Primary Wood

S = Secondary Wood

TBE = Tenon Both Ends

TOE = Tenon One End

hardware and supplies

Door Hinges	2 prs., 64mm in length
Slot-head wood screws	No. 8 x 32mm
Clout or shingle nail for backboards	38mm
Fine finish nail for mouldings	38mm

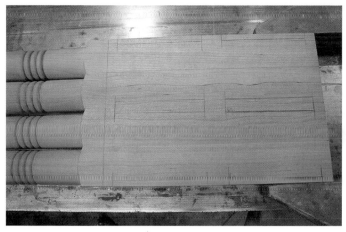

1 To begin, mill the legs, sides and back according to the cutting list. Then turn the legs according to the illustration. Mark the layout of the mortises on the upper leg area. Select the best grain pattern for the front of the piece.

2 Cut the mortises. Divide the side and back mortises into two smaller cuts; use the step method of cutting mortises by skipping every other cut and returning to clean out the sections after reaching the end of each mortise. This will prevent excessive wear on the chisel.

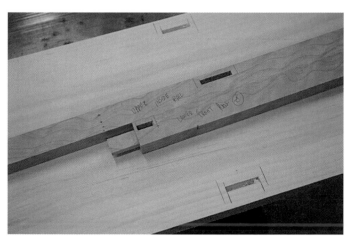

3 Don't forget to cut the mortises in the top of the upper front rail and back (for the drawer kicker), the center of the lower front rail and lower back (for the rail support) and at the ends of the lower rail for the drawer runners.

4 Test fit all pieces. If all fits are correct, proceed to assemble and glue the lower section. Glue the front and back subassemblies, then finish with the side pieces. Remember to install the drawer kicker and the support piece at this stage; they must be placed between the front rails and back of the unit.

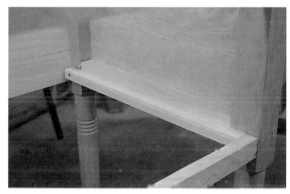

Tip Before I glue the drawer parts together, I run the bottom edge of my drawer front over the jointer with the fence set at a 5° angle and a 1/16"-deep cut. This creates a slight bevel that allows the drawer to close without the front catching on the drawer di viders. Smooth operation!

5 Tenon and glue the drawer runner into the mortise you created in the lower front rail, and nail the rear to the back leg. Nail the drawer guide to the runner, flush to the leg blocks. Be sure to level the back so the drawer will slide correctly.

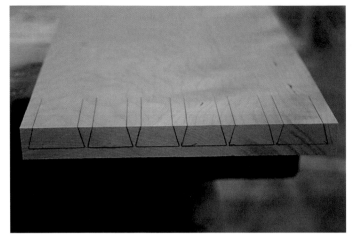

6 Build the drawer. The drawer fronts are flush with the face of the cupboard. Here you can see the layout of the hand-cut dovetails. (See "Drawer Basics: Hand-cut Dovetails" on page 8).

7 Once the drawer is built, slide it into the lower section and align the drawer front with the case front. Then measure and cut the stops for the drawer. Attach with a screw, and glue it to the back leg.

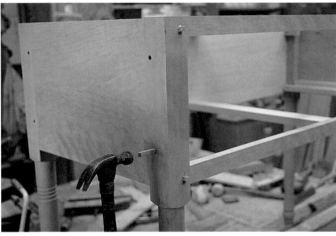

8 Remove the drawer, then lay out and drill the locations for the square pegs. Set the pegs and cut them flush with the case.

9 Mill the top of the lower section and, using a biscuit joiner, cut the recess in the sides, back and top front rail to accept the wooden clips that will hold the top in place. (See "Wood Clips" on page 8.)

10 To begin the cupboard's upper section, mill the sides and shelves to size. Lay out and cut the $1/4" \times 3/4"$-deep grooves for the shelves. Note that these are stopped dadoes that do not extend through the front of the sides. Also cut the $7/16" \times 3/4"$ rabbet for the backboards.

Tip Gang all the pieces for the job and do the layout work in one step: Assemble similar pieces simultaneously in a group, then mark them all at once.

11 Notch the front corners of the shelves to fit the stopped dado cuts.

12 Using a $\frac{1}{2}$" core box bit and another shelf as a straightedge, cut a plate groove into the back of the lower three shelves approximately $1\frac{1}{4}$" from the back edge. Make sure to begin and end short of the shelf ends.

13 Finish sand the shelves and the insides of the sides, then glue the unit together. Check for square by diagonal measurement and, when dry, add the square pegs as you did to the lower section.

14 For the doors, lay out and cut the mortises on the stiles. Because these are glass-pane doors, create a $\frac{3}{8}$" × $\frac{1}{2}$" rabbet on the interiors of all eight door pieces.

15 Cut the rails. Then set the blade height and create the appropriate tenon length on the face sides of the door-frame pieces. Cut to the depth of the rabbet cut.

16 Move the fence ⅜" closer to the blade and cut the back of the stiles as well as the outside shoulder. Then finish the tenons by completing the necessary cuts.

17 This is how the tenoned ends look after completing all cuts. Test fit all of the pieces and then assemble the door frames.

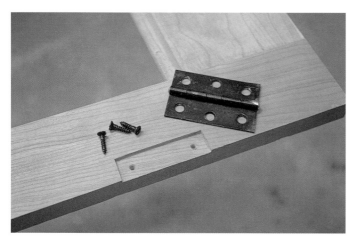

18 Rout the dadoes and install the hinges. Hang the doors and adjust the door lap to ⁵⁄₁₆". Keep the stiles equal in measurement.

19 Remove the operable door and create a ⅜" × ⅜" rabbet cut on the back side of the interior stile of the other door. (The operable door has the latching knob, the other will be opened from a release inside the cupboard.) Reinstall this door allowing the rabbet to overlap onto the opposite door.

20 Mark the location on the latched door and create a matching rabbet on this door, producing the half-lap joint shown here.

21 With the doors installed, mark the top and bottom of each shelf on the door stiles. Also mark for a ¾"-wide vertical divider on the edge of the two rails of each door. This will align the glass dividers on the door.

22 Cut the pieces ¼" × ½" for the interior and the pieces ¼" × ¾" for the exterior glass dividers. With the door facedown, fit and glue the interior horizontal pieces, allowing them to rest on the lip created by the rabbet cut on the door pieces.

23 Flip the door so it's face up, and fit the long vertical exterior piece into the center of the opening. Glue this to the two previously installed pieces. These three pieces form the basis of the door's glass grid.

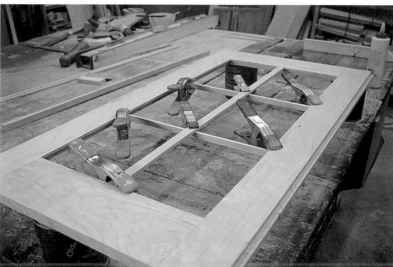

24 Cut, fit and install the remaining pieces necessary to complete the door. Then repeat the procedure on the other door.

25 When the upper unit is dry, mill the top and bottom front case pieces a bit longer than required, sand the insides and glue them to the upper unit. After the glue dries, drill and install the square pegs. (By allowing the glue to dry, you reduce the risk of breakout.) Cut the extra length flush with the side of the case.

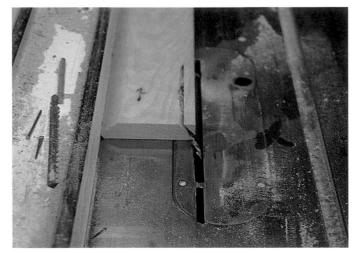

26 Make the crown moulding according to the illustration. Set the blade to 40° and make the first cut with the board face against the fence. The fence is set on the left side of the blade. Then, set the fence to the right side of the blade, and lay the face flat on the table saw in order to cut the complementary angle on the opposite edge of the board, achieving 90°.

27 With the settings the same as in step 26, cut the angled edge on the bottom moulding of the upper section. Sand both mouldings, progressing to 180-grit sandpaper.

28 Sand the outside of the case to 180 grit, then fit the crown moulding to the case and attach with a reproduction finish nail. Dowel the top edge of the crown from the side into the front piece and sand smooth.

29 Align the bottom moulding with the inside of the front and sides of the case. Make the 45° cuts at the front corners, square cut the back corners and attach with No. 8 × 1¼" slot-head wood screws into the sides. Glue and screw the moulding to the front. Then dowel the front corners as you did on the crown moulding.

30 Cut the half-lap joints on the backboards. Then final sand the pieces.

31 Mark both sides of the interior stile on the operable door. Using a biscuit joiner, cut the ¼" slot in the bottom of the second shelf to accept the catch shown here. After applying the selected finish, align the catch with the slot and install with a No. 8 × 1¼" slot-head wood screw.

32 This is what the latching knob looks like. The project is now ready to move on to the finishing stage.

33 After the finishing is complete, attach the top using wooden clips. The finish I selected for the cupboard is lacquer. (See "Lacquer Finishing" on page 93.)

34 Nail the backboards into place using reproduction nails, then install the glass into the doors. On this cupboard, I used Bendheim's Light Restoration Glass (see page 2 for contact information).

Tip Use water putty for installing glass panes into the doors. Water putty gives a yellowed look that simulates age. I use Durham's Rock Hard Water Putty.

shaker SEWING DESK

MANY YEARS AGO, I ATTENDED AN ANTIQUE SHOW AT THE famous Round Stone Barn in Hancock Shaker Village in Massachusetts. There, I happened upon an original Shaker sewing desk. Each community built its own version of the sewing desk. Although I cannot remember from which community this antique came, I do remember being in great awe of it.

The desk was to be used by two Shaker "sisters" as they sewed. One sister would use the side bank of drawers, while the other used the drawers in front; the two sisters would share the upper bank.

My version of this striking desk is based on an 1840s piece created in the Shaker community of Canterbury, New Hampshire, and it already has made an appearance at the Round Stone Barn. I hope your version of this desk makes an appearance in the future.

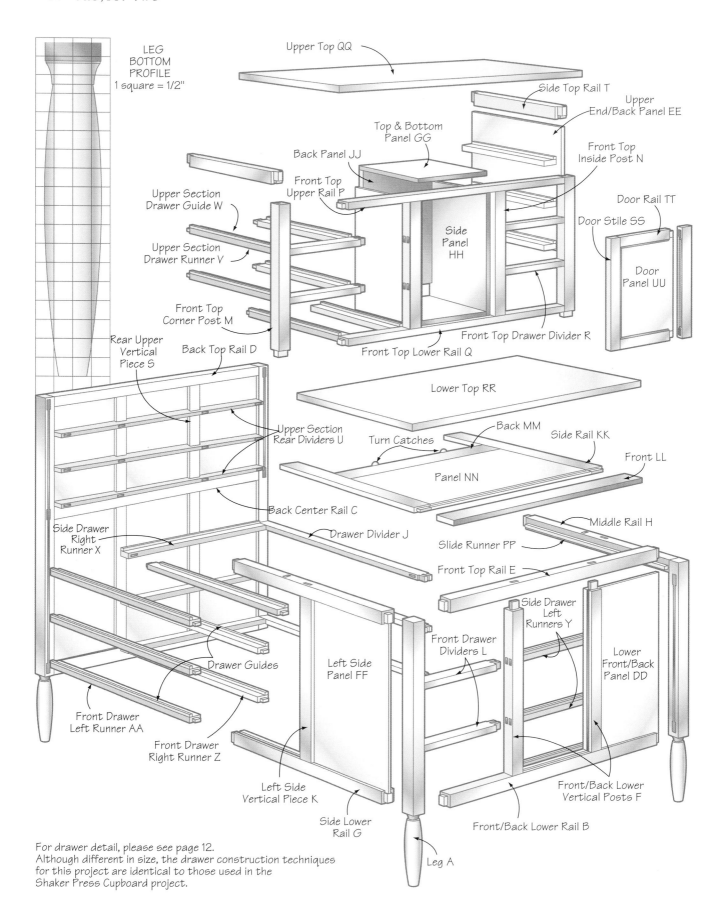

LEG
BOTTOM
PROFILE
1 square = 1/2"

Upper Top QQ

Side Top Rail T

Upper
End/Back Panel EE

Top & Bottom
Panel GG

Back Panel JJ

Front Top
Upper Rail P

Front Top
Inside Post N

Upper Section
Drawer Guide W

Side
Panel
HH

Door Rail TT

Door Stile SS

Upper Section
Drawer Runner V

Door
Panel UU

Front Top
Corner Post M

Front Top Drawer Divider R

Front Top Lower Rail Q

Rear Upper
Vertical
Piece S

Back Top Rail D

Lower Top RR

Upper Section
Rear Dividers U

Back MM

Side Rail KK

Turn Catches

Front LL

Panel NN

Back Center Rail C

Middle Rail H

Drawer Divider J

Slide Runner PP

Side Drawer
Right
Runner X

Front Top Rail E

Side Drawer
Left
Runners Y

Front Drawer
Dividers L

Lower
Front/Back
Panel DD

Drawer Guides

Left Side
Panel FF

Front Drawer
Left Runner AA

Front Drawer
Right Runner Z

Left Side
Vertical Piece K

Front/Back Lower
Vertical Posts F

Side Lower
Rail G

Front/Back Lower Rail B

Leg A

For drawer detail, please see page 12.
Although different in size, the drawer construction techniques
for this project are identical to those used in the
Shaker Press Cupboard project.

cutting list | inches

SHAKER SEWING DESK

REFERENCE	QUANTITY	PART	STOCK	THICKNESS	WIDTH	LENGTH	COMMENTS
A	4	Legs	P	$1^1/_2$	$1^1/_2$	$41^3/_4$	see instructions
B	2	Front and Back Lower Rails	P	$1^1/_4$	$1^1/_2$	$30^1/_4$	$^7/_8$" TBE
C	1	Back Center Rail	P	$1^1/_2$	$1^1/_2$	$30^1/_4$	$^7/_8$" TBE
D	1	Back Top Rail	P	1	$1^1/_2$	$30^1/_4$	$^7/_8$" TBE
E	1	Front Top Rail	P	$^3/_4$	$1^1/_2$	$30^1/_4$	$^7/_8$" TBE
F	4	Front and Back Lower Vertical Posts	P	$1^1/_2$	$1^1/_2$	$18^1/_4$	$^7/_8$" TBE
G	2	L & R Side Lower Rails	P	$1^1/_4$	$1^1/_2$	$25^3/_4$	$^7/_8$" TBE
H	2	L & R Middle Rails	P	$1^1/_2$	$1^1/_2$	$25^3/_4$	$^7/_8$" TBE
J	2	Right Side Drawer Dividers	P	$^3/_4$	$1^1/_2$	$25^3/_4$	$^7/_8$" TBE
K	1	Left Side Vertical Piece	P	$1^1/_2$	$1^1/_2$	$18^1/_4$	$^7/_8$" TBE
L	2	Front Drawer Dividers	P	$^3/_4$	$1^1/_2$	$10^1/_4$	$^7/_8$" TBE
M	2	Front Top Corner Posts	P	$1^1/_2$	$1^1/_2$	$13^3/_8$	
N	2	Front Top Inside Posts	P	$1^1/_2$	$1^1/_2$	$10^1/_4$	
P	1	Front Top Upper Rail	P	$^5/_8$	$1^1/_2$	$30^1/_4$	$^7/_8$" TBE
Q	1	Front Top Lower Rail	P	$^3/_4$	$1^1/_2$	$30^1/_4$	$^7/_8$" TBE
R	4	Front Top Drawer Dividers	P	$^5/_8$	$1^1/_2$	$10^1/_4$	$^7/_8$" TBE
S	2	Rear Upper Vertical Pcs.	P	$1^1/_2$	$1^1/_2$	$13^1/_4$	$^7/_8$" TBE
T	2	Side Top Rails	P	1	$1^1/_2$	$10^1/_4$	$^7/_8$" TBE
U	3	Upper Section Rear Dividers	S	$^5/_8$	$^7/_8$	$29^1/_2$	
V	12	Upper Section Drawer Runners	S	$^5/_8$	$^7/_8$	$8^5/_{16}$	$^3/_8$" TBE
W	12	Upper Section Drawer Guides	S	$^1/_4$	$^7/_8$	$6^1/_2$	
X	3	Side Drawer Right Runners	S	$^3/_4$	$1^1/_8$	$22^3/_8$	$^3/_8$" TOE
Y	3	Side Drawer Left Runners	S	$^3/_4$	$1^1/_8$	$19^3/_4$	$^3/_8$" TOE
Z	3	Front Drawer Right Runners	S	$^3/_4$	$1^1/_8$	$23^5/_8$	$^3/_8$" TOE
AA	3	Front Drawer Left Runners	S	$^3/_4$	$1^1/_8$	25	$^3/_8$" TOE
BB	9	Lower Section Drawer Guides	S	$^1/_4$	1	16	attach to runners
CC	3	Lower Section Drawer Guides	S	$^3/_8$	$^3/_4$	16	nail to rails

FLAT PANELS

REFERENCE	QUANTITY	PART	STOCK	THICKNESS	WIDTH	LENGTH	COMMENTS
DD	5	Lower Front and Back Panels	P	$^5/_8$	9	$17^1/_8$	$^3/_8$" rabbet AS
EE	5	Upper End and Back Panels	P	$^5/_8$	9	$12^1/_8$	$^3/_8$" rabbet AS
FF	2	Left Side Panels	P	$^5/_8$	$11^3/_4$	$17^1/_8$	$^3/_8$" rabbet AS

CENTRAL CUPBOARD PIECES

GG	2	Top and Bottom Panels	S	$^3/_8$	$8^3/_8$	$7^1/_2$	
HH	2	Side Panels	S	$^3/_8$	7	$10^1/_4$	
JJ	1	Back Panel	S	$^3/_8$	$9^1/_{16}$	$10^1/_4$	

SLIDING WORK SURFACE PIECES

KK	2	Side Rails	P	$^3/_4$	$2^3/_4$	$22^1/_4$	1" TOE
LL	1	Front	P	$^3/_4$	$2^3/_4$	$28^3/_8$	
MM	1	Back	P	$^3/_4$	$2^3/_4$	$24^7/_8$	1" TBE
NN	1	Panel	P	$^3/_4$	$9^1/_8$	$23^1/_2$	$^1/_4$" × $^3/_8$" TAS
PP	2	Slide Runners	S	$^5/_8$	$^3/_4$	16	
QQ	1	Upper Top	P	$^3/_4$	$13^3/_4$	34	
RR	1	Lower Top	P	$^3/_4$	$17^1/_2$	34	

CUPBOARD DOOR

SS	2	Door Stiles	P	$^3/_4$	$1^3/_4$	$10^1/_4$	
TT	2	Door Rails	P	$^3/_4$	$1^3/_4$	$6^3/_4$	1" TBE
UU	1	Door Panel	P	$^1/_2$	$5^3/_8$	$7^1/_4$	$^1/_4$" rabbet AS

DRAWER PARTS

VV	6	Drawer Fronts	P	$^{13}/_{16}$	$3^1/_4$	$9^1/_4$	$^1/_2$" × $^3/_8$" rabbet three sides
WW	3	Drawer Fronts	P	$^{13}/_{16}$	$5^1/_4$	$9^1/_4$	$^1/_2$" × $^3/_8$" rabbet three sides
XX	3	Drawer Fronts	P	$^{13}/_{16}$	$5^1/_4$	$24^3/_4$	$^1/_2$" × $^3/_8$" rabbet three sides
YY	12	Drawer Sides	S	$^3/_8$	$2^1/_8$	$9^1/_4$	
ZZ	12	Drawer Sides	S	$^3/_8$	$4^7/_8$	$16^3/_4$	
AAA	6	Drawer Backs	S	$^3/_8$	$2^1/_8$	$8^7/_8$	
BBB	3	Drawer Backs	S	$^3/_8$	$4^1/_8$	$8^7/_{16}$	
CCC	3	Drawer Backs	S	$^3/_8$	$4^1/_8$	$23^{15}/_{16}$	
DDD	6	Drawer Bottoms	S	$^1/_2$	$9^1/_2$	$8^1/_2$	
EEE	3	Drawer Bottoms	S	$^5/_8$	$17^1/_4$	$8^1/_2$	
FFF	3	Drawer Bottoms	S	$^5/_8$	$17^1/_4$	24	

hardware and supplies

Shaker wooden knobs	15 knobs, $1^1/_4$" in length
Standard butt hinge	1 pr., 1"
Wood screws	No. 8 × $1^1/_4$"
Knobs from Horton Brasses, Inc.	2 H-42 knobs, $^1/_2$" with wood screws
Full-mortise lock from Woodcraft Supply	
Nails	

TBE = Tenon Both Ends

TOE = Tenon One End

AS = All Sides

TAS = Tenon All Sides

P = Primary Wood

S = Secondary Wood

cutting list | millimeters

SHAKER SEWING DESK

REFERENCE	QUANTITY	PART	STOCK	THICKNESS	WIDTH	LENGTH	COMMENTS
A	4	Legs	P	38	38	1060	see instructions
B	2	Front and Back Lower Rails	P	32	38	768	22mm TBE
C	1	Back Center Rail	P	38	38	768	22mm TBE
D	1	Back Top Rail	P	25	38	768	22mm TBE
E	1	Front Top Rail	P	19	38	768	22mm TBE
F	4	Front and Back Lower Vertical Posts	P	38	38	463	22mm TBE
G	2	L & R Side Lower Rails	P	32	38	654	22mm TBE
H	2	L & R Middle Rails	P	38	38	654	22mm TBE
J	2	Right Side Drawer Dividers	P	19	38	654	22mm TBE
K	1	Left Side Vertical Piece	P	38	38	463	22mm TBE
L	2	Front Drawer Dividers	P	19	38	260	22mm TBE
M	2	Front Top Corner Posts	P	38	38	340	
N	2	Front Top Inside Posts	P	38	38	260	
P	1	Front Top Upper Rail	P	16	38	268	22mm TBE
Q	1	Front Top Lower Rail	P	19	38	268	22mm TBE
R	4	Front Top Drawer Dividers	P	16	38	260	22mm TBE
S	2	Rear Upper Vertical Pcs.	P	38	38	336	22mm TBE
T	2	Side Top Rails	P	25	38	260	22mm TBE
U	3	Upper Section Rear Dividers	S	16	22	750	
V	12	Upper Section Drawer Runners	S	16	22	211	10mm TBE
W	12	Upper Section Drawer Guides	S	6	22	165	
X	3	Side Drawer Right Runners	S	19	29	569	10mm TOE
Y	3	Side Dwr. Left Runners	S	19	29	502	10mm TOE
Z	3	Front Drawer Right Runners	S	19	29	600	10mm TOE
AA	3	Front Drawer Left Runners	S	19	29	635	10mm TOE
BB	9	Lower Section Drawer Guides	S	6	25	406	attach to runners
CC	3	Lower Section Drawer Guides	S	10	19	406	nail to rails

FLAT PANELS

REFERENCE	QUANTITY	PART	STOCK	THICKNESS	WIDTH	LENGTH	COMMENTS
DD	5	Lower Front and Back Panels	P	16	229	435	10mm rabbet AS
EE	5	Upper End and Back Panels	P	16	229	308	10mm rabbet AS
FF	2	Left Side Panels	P	16	298	435	10mm rabbet AS

CENTRAL CUPBOARD PIECES

GG	2	Top and Bottom Panels	S	10	213	191	
HH	2	Side Panels	S	10	178	260	
JJ	1	Back Panel	S	10	231	260	

SLIDING WORK SURFACE PIECES

KK	2	Side Rails	P	19	70	565	25mm TOE
LL	1	Front	P	19	70	721	
MM	1	Back	P	19	70	642	25mm TBE
NN	1	Panel	P	19	232	597	6mm × 10mm TAS
PP	2	Slide Runners	S	16	19	406	
QQ	1	Upper Top	P	19	349	864	
RR	1	Lower Top	P	19	445	864	

CUPBOARD DOOR

SS	2	Door Stiles	P	19	45	260	
TT	2	Door Rails	P	19	45	165	25mm TBE
UU	1	Door Panel	P	13	137	184	6mm rabbet AS

DRAWER PARTS

VV	6	Drawer Fronts	P	21	82	235	13mm × 10mm rabbet three sides
WW	3	Drawer Fronts	P	21	133	235	13mm × 10mm rabbet three sides
XX	3	Drawer Fronts	P	21	133	629	13mm × 10mm rabbet three sides
YY	12	Drawer Sides	S	10	73	235	
ZZ	12	Drawer Sides	S	10	124	425	
AAA	6	Drawer Backs	S	10	54	225	
BBB	3	Drawer Backs	S	10	105	214	
CCC	3	Drawer Backs	S	10	105	608	
DDD	6	Drawer Bottoms	S	13	242	216	
EEE	3	Drawer Bottoms	S	16	438	216	
FFF	3	Drawer Bottoms	S	16	438	610	

hardware and supplies

Shaker wooden knobs	15 knobs, 32mm in length
Standard butt hinge	1 pr., 25mm
Wood screws	No. 8 × 32mm
Knobs from Horton Brasses, Inc.	2 H-42 knobs, 13mm with wood screws
Full-mortise lock from Woodcraft Supply	
Nails	

TBE = Tenon Both Ends

TOE = Tenon One End

AS = All Sides

TAS = Tenon All Sides

P = Primary Wood

S = Secondary Wood

1 | Mill the four leg posts and rails for all sides. Include the vertical pieces for the front, back and left sides. Turn the legs to size according to the plan, trim the rear posts to $40\frac{3}{4}$" and cut the front posts to $28\frac{1}{4}$". The off-fall will be cut to $13\frac{3}{8}$" for the front top corner posts.

2 | Begin with the front legs and vertical pieces for the case front. Lay out and cut the mortises (set $\frac{1}{4}$" from the front side) for the top rail ($\frac{3}{4}$" below the top of the post) to leave room for the slide-out work surface and the lower rail. Remember that the left front leg also gets mortised for the front drawer dividers, which are double tenoned as shown above.

3 | Lay out and cut the front top and bottom rails for the mortises for the vertical front pieces. One vertical piece also will be mortised for the front drawer dividers.

4 | Cut the matching tenons on all of the front frame pieces. You will have two long rails and two short drawer dividers that are double tenons, as well as two vertical pieces that are tenoned into the top and bottom rails.

Tip With a piece that has a large number of mortise-and-tenon joints, such as the sewing desk in this chapter, I find that after I have made my cheek cuts on the table saw, I use the back edge of a featherboard kit to act as a stop for finishing my shoulder cuts on the band saw.

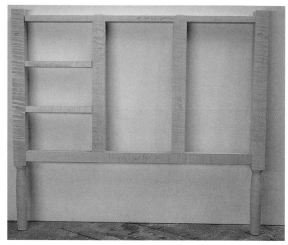

5 | This is a close-up of how the double tenons look. The one on the right is a completed tenon.

6 | Temporarily assemble the front frame, mark the locations on the mortises for the drawer runners, and scribe a pencil line around all four sides where the panels will fit. Repeat this process for the two sides and the back of the desk.

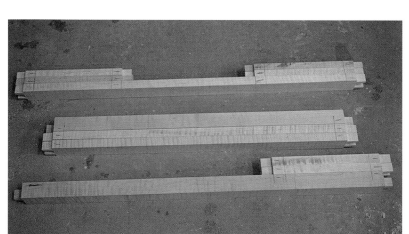

7 | After you have created all of the mortises and tenons on the rails and intermediate vertical pieces, and have marked the locations on the front and right side drawer dividers, cut the mortises for the drawer runners.

8 | Using a dado blade, create the $\frac{1}{4}" \times \frac{3}{8}"$ groove for the panels in all appropriate areas; this includes the posts which are drop-cut, the vertical pieces on all sides, the intermediate rail on the back, and the top and bottom rails on all sides (except the right).

9 | Notice here that the ⅜" × ¾" tenons and the ¼" × ⅜" groove for the panels are all set ¼" from the front edge.

10 | Cut ¼" off the inside edges of the front vertical piece located between the two panels, the piece located directly opposite on the back frame, as well as the middle piece on the left side. This will allow for the installation of the drawer guides.

11 | Mill the panels to size and cut a ⅜" × ⅜" rabbet on all sides. Final sand these panels.

12 | With all the pieces complete, it is time to assemble the front and back. Glue all mortise-and-tenon joints; be sure to allow the panels to float. When they are dry, assemble the sides and glue only the front mortise-and-tenon joints. Do not glue the rear mortise-and-tenon joints at this time.

13 After you have cut the mortise-and-tenon joints for the front upper drawer section, mortise for the door hinge in the inner right vertical post. The two inner posts, which are attached with screws, fit between the upper and lower rails. Those rails mortise into the corner posts with the double tenons. Don't forget the mortises for the drawer runners. Once the joinery for the drawer dividers is complete, assemble the upper section.

14 Glue the upper front drawer section into the mortises created in the top rails of both the right and left sides. When attaching this section, it is important to keep it at 90° with the side top rails. Don't worry about installing the flat panels into the top section at this time.

15 Transfer the drawer runner locations from the front dividers to the upper section rear drawer supports. Using a square, locate the position of the support on the case back.

16 Cut the mortises for the runners and remove the case back. Then glue and nail the rear drawer supports onto the case back at those locations, centered from side to side. These pieces will accept the small drawer runners when the final assembly is completed.

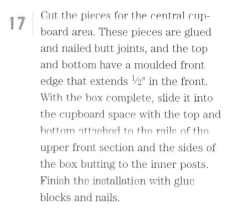

17 Cut the pieces for the central cupboard area. These pieces are glued and nailed butt joints, and the top and bottom have a moulded front edge that extends ½" in the front. With the box complete, slide it into the cupboard space with the top and bottom attached to the rails of the upper front section and the sides of the box butting to the inner posts. Finish the installation with glue blocks and nails.

18 Make the upper section drawer runners by cutting to size and milling the ¼" × ⅝" × ⅜" tenons on both ends. Once milled, add the drawer guides to the pieces, making six matching pairs like those shown above. Install the runners/guides, then remove and number them.

19 This is a tricky step, so it is helpful to have another set of hands at this stage. Apply glue to the runners/guides and to the side/rear mortises and tenons, then make the final connection. Clamp and let dry. There are six joints for the two sides and 24 mortise-and-tenon joints for the small drawer dividers.

21 After the case has dried, install the square pegs where necessary.

20 Here you see the two remaining flat panels being installed into the sides. Once in place, glue the upper section top rail into its final position.

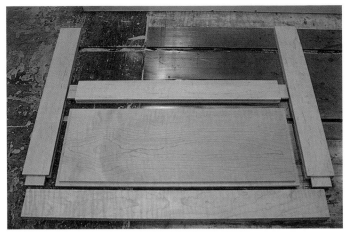

22 Make the sliding work surface. Install the rear panel support into the sides, slide the floating panel in, and attach the side runners into the front. This allows the exposed front an uninterrupted view.

23 Cut the lower area drawer runners to size. The right-side drawer runners that attach to the case back need to have a mortise cut into them to allow support for the right side runner on the front drawers. With the mortises cut, apply the ¼"-thick guides to all runners except those that attach to the lower case rails (two for the right-side drawers and one for the front drawers). The guides for these runners are pieces cut to fit between the vertical posts that nail directly onto the case lower rails.

24 Install the lower area runners/guides. Begin by installing the left runners of both the front and right-side drawers. The mortises are glued and the runners are nailed into the vertical pieces where they lap.

25 Now install the balance of the runners. However, you need to assemble the mortise-and-tenon joint of the two runners first, then maneuver the other tenons into their appropriate mortises. When they are complete, nail those pieces to the vertical posts, as well.

26 Build the drawers. Shown here are the lipped drawer fronts. (See "Drawer Basics: Hand-cut Dovetails" on page 8.)

27 Install the slide runners by nailing them into the lower section's top side rails, and fit the finished sliding work surface into place. Notice the small turn catches that keep the slide from sliding out completely. They are installed with screws and turned sideways to install the slide. Once in, the pins are turned downward and act as a catch on the front rail.

28 Mill the lower top, and cut the notches at each side at the back so the rear of the top will slide under the upper section lower rail. Final sand the top and all areas that will become inaccessible after the top is installed. Attach with screws from beneath into the lower rail of the upper section.

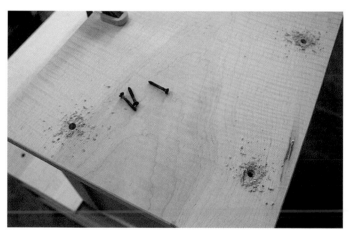

29 Mill, cut and final sand the upper section top. Install (along with the lower top) by counterboring for a ⅜" plug and screwing the tops into the corresponding rails. Then insert the plug.

30 Build and install the cupboard-area door as shown here. Create the moulded inner edge, and mill the haunched mortise-and-tenon joints. Next, cut the inner edge to fit the 45° angle at the corners, and groove to receive the rabbeted flat panel. Mortise the stile for a full-mortise lock, and mill for the hinges. Don't forget the strike plate for the lock.

31 Final sand all surfaces and apply your selected finish. I used a "flattened shellac with glaze," but eliminated the final coat of lacquer and simply waxed the surface. (See "Flattened Shellac with Glaze Finish" on page 105.)

mt. lebanon SHAKER COUNTER

WITH ITS CLEAN AND SIMPLISTIC LINES, THIS PIECE OF FINE Shaker furniture definitely caught my eye. Because of all the wonderful storage space available, this piece is a great addition to the home.

Based on a circa-1860 eight-drawer chest attributed to Brother Amos Stewart, it is believed to have been used as a tailoring counter. This chest displays frame-and-panel ends with dovetailed drawer dividers, as well as other characteristics of Shaker craftsmanship, such as the use of a diagonally sawn piece to complete the foot.

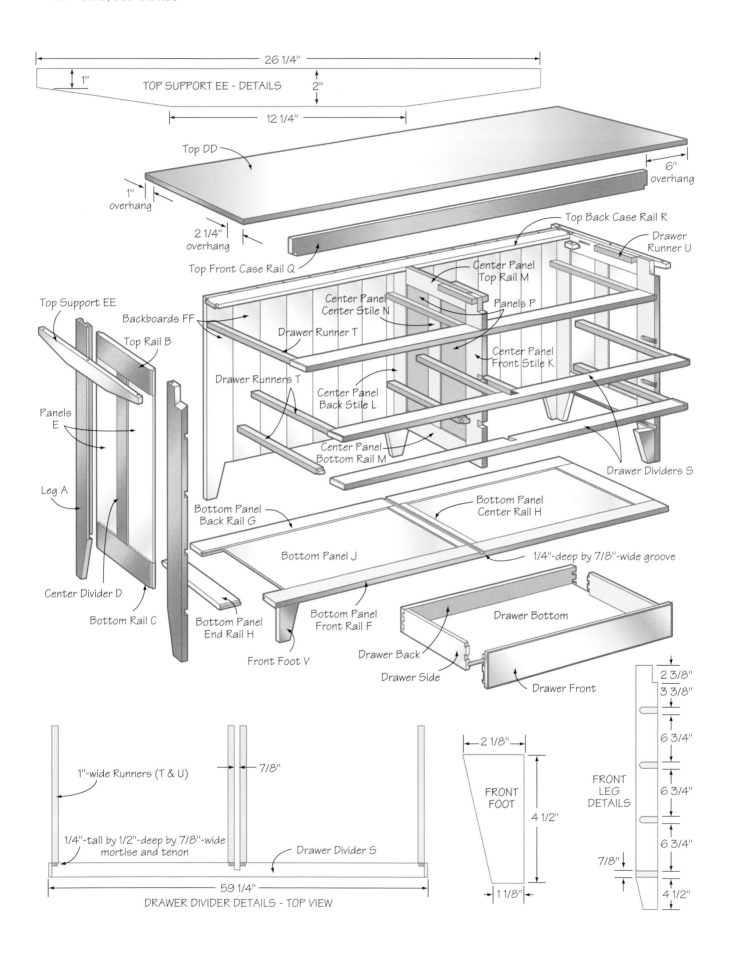

TOP SUPPORT EE - DETAILS

26 1/4"

1"

2"

12 1/4"

Top DD

6" overhang

1" overhang

2 1/4" overhang

Top Back Case Rail R

Drawer Runner U

Top Front Case Rail Q

Center Panel Top Rail M

Panels P

Top Support EE

Center Panel Center Stile N

Backboards FF

Top Rail B

Drawer Runner T

Center Panel Front Stile K

Panels E

Drawer Runners T

Center Panel Back Stile L

Leg A

Center Panel Bottom Rail M

Drawer Dividers S

Center Divider D

Bottom Panel Back Rail G

Bottom Panel Center Rail H

Bottom Rail C

Bottom Panel J

1/4"-deep by 7/8"-wide groove

Bottom Panel End Rail H

Bottom Panel Front Rail F

Drawer Bottom

Front Foot V

Drawer Back

Drawer Side

Drawer Front

1"-wide Runners (T & U)

7/8"

2 3/8"

3 3/8"

6 3/4"

2 1/8"

FRONT FOOT

4 1/2"

FRONT LEG DETAILS

6 3/4"

6 3/4"

1/4"-tall by 1/2"-deep by 7/8"-wide mortise and tenon

Drawer Divider S

7/8"

59 1/4"

1 1/8"

4 1/2"

DRAWER DIVIDER DETAILS - TOP VIEW

cutting list | inches

MT. LEBANON SHAKER COUNTER

SIDE PANELS

REFERENCE	QUANTITY	PART	STOCK	THICKNESS	WIDTH	LENGTH	COMMENTS
A	4	Legs	P	$1/8$	3	$34^1/8$	
B	2	Top Rails	P	$7/8$	3	$21^1/2$	$1^1/4$" TBE
C	2	Bottom Rails	P	$7/8$	$3^1/4$	$21^1/2$	$1^1/4$" TBE
D	2	Center Dividers	P	$7/8$	3	$25^3/4$	$1^1/4$" TBE
E	4	Panels	P	$9/16$	$8^5/8$	$23^7/8$	$3/8$" TAS

BOTTOM PANELS

F	1	Front Rail	P	$7/8$	$2^3/4$	$58^5/8$	
G	1	Back Rail	S	$7/8$	$2^3/4$	$58^5/8$	
H	3	Center, End Rails	S	$7/8$	$2^3/4$	$21^1/4$	$1^1/4$" TBE
J	2	Panels	S	$7/8$	$19^3/8$	$25^{13}/16$	$3/8$" TAS

CENTER PARTITION

K	1	Front Stile	P	$7/8$	$2^3/4$	$28^7/8$	
L	1	Back Stile	S	$7/8$	$2^3/4$	$28^7/8$	
M	2	Top, Bottom Rails	S	$7/8$	$2^3/4$	$21^1/4$	$1^1/4$" TBE
N	1	Center Stile	S	$7/8$	$2^3/4$	$25^7/8$	$1^1/4$" TBE
P	2	Panels	S	$7/8$	$8^5/8$	24	$3/8$" TAS
Q	1	Top Front Case Rail	P	$7/8$	$2^3/8$	$59^7/8$	
R	1	Top Back Case Rail	S	$7/8$	$2^1/4$	$59^1/8$	
S	3	Drawer Dividers	P	$7/8$	$2^1/4$	$59^1/8$	
T	8	Drawer Runners	S	$7/8$	1	22	$1/2$" TOE
U	4	Drawer Runners	S	$7/8$	1	12	$1/2$" TOE
V	2	Front Feet	P	$7/8$	$2^1/8$	$4^1/2$	

DRAWER PARTS

W	2	Drawer Fronts	P	$13/16$	$3^7/8$	$29^1/4$	$3/8$" lip three sides
X	6	Drawer Fronts	P	$13/16$	7	$29^1/4$	$3/8$" lip three sides
Y	12	Drawer Sides	S	$9/16$	$6^5/8$	20	large
Z	4	Drawer Sides	S	$9/16$	$3^1/4$	20	small
AA	6	Drawer Backs	S	$9/16$	$5^7/8$	$28^1/2$	large
BB	2	Drawer Backs	S	$9/16$	$2^1/2$	$28^1/2$	small
CC	8	Drawer Bottoms	S	$9/16$	$20^1/4$	$27^3/4$	
DD	1	Top	P	$13/16$	$71^7/8$	28	
EE	2	Top Supports	P	$7/8$	2	$26^1/4$	
FF		Backboards*	S	$5/8$	59	30	many pieces

*I allow three of the series of backboards to extend $3/4$" to act as legs. Place one at each end, with a center leg.

TBE = Tenon Both Ends

TAS = Tenon All Sides

TOE = Tenon One End

P = Primary Wood

S = Secondary Wood

hardware and supplies

Wooden knobs	4, $1^1/4$" diameter
Wooden knobs	12, 2" diameter
Nails	40, $1^1/2$" clout or shingle
Screws	12, No. 8 $\times$ $1^1/4$"

cutting list | millimeters

MT. LEBANON SHAKER COUNTER

SIDE PANELS

REFERENCE	QUANTITY	PART	STOCK	THICKNESS	WIDTH	LENGTH	COMMENTS
A	4	Legs	P	22	76	867	
B	2	Top Rails	P	22	76	546	32mm TBE
C	2	Bottom Rails	P	22	82	546	32mm TBE
D	2	Center Dividers	P	22	76	648	32mm TBE
E	4	Panels	P	14	219	606	10mm TAS

BOTTOM PANELS

REFERENCE	QUANTITY	PART	STOCK	THICKNESS	WIDTH	LENGTH	COMMENTS
F	1	Front Rail	P	22	70	1489	
G	1	Back Rail	S	22	70	1489	
H	3	Center, End Rails	S	22	70	539	32mm TBE
J	2	Panels	S	22	493	640	10mm TAS

CENTER PARTITION

REFERENCE	QUANTITY	PART	STOCK	THICKNESS	WIDTH	LENGTH	COMMENTS
K	1	Front Stile	P	22	70	733	
L	1	Back Stile	S	22	70	733	
M	2	Top, Bottom Rails	S	22	70	539	32mm TBE
N	1	Center Stile	S	22	70	657	32mm TBE
P	2	Panels	S	22	219	610	10mm TAS
Q	1	Top Front Case Rail	P	22	61	1521	
R	1	Top Back Case Rail	S	22	57	1502	
S	3	Drawer Dividers	S	22	57	1502	
T	8	Drawer Runners	S	22	25	559	13mm TOE
U	4	Drawer Runners	S	22	25	305	13mm TOE
V	2	Front Feet	P	22	54	115	

DRAWER PARTS

REFERENCE	QUANTITY	PART	STOCK	THICKNESS	WIDTH	LENGTH	COMMENTS
W	2	Drawer Fronts	P	21	98	743	10mm lip three sides
X	6	Drawer Fronts	P	21	178	743	10mm lip three sides
Y	12	Drawer Sides	S	14	168	508	large
Z	4	Drawer Sides	S	14	82	508	small
AA	6	Drawer Backs	S	14	149	724	large
BB	2	Drawer Backs	S	14	64	724	small
CC	8	Drawer Bottoms	S	14	514	705	
DD	1	Top	P	21	1825	711	
EE	2	Top Supports	P	22	51	666	
FF		Backboards*	S	16	1499	762	many pieces

*I allow three of the series of backboards to extend 19mm to act as legs. Place one at each end, with a center leg.

TBE = Tenon Both Ends

TAS = Tenon All Sides

TOE = Tenon One End

P = Primary Wood

S = Secondary Wood

hardware and supplies

Wooden knobs	4, 32mm diameter
Wooden knobs	12, 51mm diameter
Nails	40, 38mm clout or shingle
Screws	12, No. 8 × 32mm

1 | After cutting your end panel pieces to size, cut the appropriate mortise-and-tenon joinery for the center dividers and where the upper and lower rails meet the legs.

2 | Cut the grooves to receive the flat panels. Mark the beginning and ending cut points with masking tape. Set the blade to cut $\frac{3}{8}$" deep and the fence at $\frac{5}{16}$". Drop cut the piece onto the blade at the start of the mortise, then extend the cut to the far end of the second mortise. Reverse the piece and repeat the same procedure. This ensures that the groove is located in the exact center of the workpiece.

3 | Groove all legs, rails and center stiles on both sides.

4 | Make the flat panels by rabbeting all sides of the panel with a $\frac{5}{16}$" × $\frac{3}{8}$" rabbet, leaving a $\frac{1}{4}$" tongue.

5 | I chose the table saw for this operation, but a router with a rabbet bit is also a good choice.

6 | Preassemble all parts to check for fit. It is important at this time to sand the flat panels to 180 grit. If it all fits, apply glue into the mortises and glue the tenons only, making sure not to glue the panels. The panels will be able to float in the grooves.

7 After the glue has set, create a ¾" × ⅜" rabbet to receive the backboards and a ⅞" × ¼" groove to accept the bottom. Create the groove exactly at the bottom of the lower rail on each end panel unit.

oil/varnish finishing

Sand all parts to 180 grit. Knock off any sharp corners with 120-grit sandpaper, then apply the selected finish. Here I use an oil/varnish finish that is a mixture of one-third turpentine, one-third boiled linseed oil and one-third spar varnish. It is applied with a brush to all visible areas (not the interior parts), allowed to become tacky to the touch and wiped clean. It takes about three coats. Each coat adds a bit more sheen and durability.

Once the finish is dry, apply a coat of paste wax with #0000 steel wool. Buff with a clean cloth. The wax is equal parts beeswax, turpentine and boiled linseed oil melted to the consistency of soft butter in a double boiler. Adjustments may be made to achieve the desired consistency. Use caution when heating this mixture.

8 Cut the slot for the dovetail drawer dividers (which extend 2¼" into the legs) and the half-pin cut for the top front case rail.

9 Don't forget the top back case rail dovetail.

10 The center partition and bottom panel are both constructed in the same manner. The only difference is size and the orientation of the middle stiles. The middle stile on the center partition is parallel to the front stile. On the bottom panel, the middle stile is perpendicular to the front stile. Use the primary hardwood for the front stile on both units.

11 On the table saw, cut the mortise-and-tenon joints and run the grooves to accept the floating panels as before. Then create a tongue on each of the panel's four sides to fit. Shown above is a finished panel (the top panel in the photograph) and a panel with only the first cuts made (the bottom panel in the photograph).

12 Fit all pieces on both units, then glue all mortise-and-tenon joints. When dry and sanded, slide the bottom panel into the grooves in the end panels. It is easiest to do this with the piece upside down. Align the front edges. Nail the bottom panel to the end panel in the rabbeted area that was created between the feet when you made the dado.

14 Notch the top rear of the center partition where the top case rails will be affixed. Then lay out and cut the half-lap joint for the intermediate drawer dividers. (This cut should be $7/8$" tall × $1\,1/8$" deep.) I use a straightedge to lay out the locations.

13 Cut a $1/4$" × $7/8$" dado in the center of the bottom panel into which the center partition will go.

15 Glue and attach the center partition into the bottom panel with No. 8 × $1\,1/4$" screws from the underside. Then glue the front and nail the top back case rail into place and allow to dry. Pay careful attention in order to exactly center the partition in the case!

16 Cut and mill the drawer dividers to length, and form the corresponding dovetail on each end to fit into the appropriate opening in the case sides. Slide the drawer dividers into the dovetailed slots in the case sides and also into the notched areas in the center partition. Mark the location of the half-lap onto the divider. Then finish the half-lap joint so that it is flush to the case front.

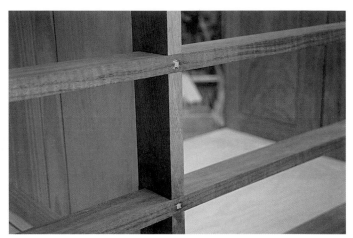

17 With the dividers removed, lay out and cut the $\frac{1}{4}" \times \frac{7}{8}" \times \frac{1}{2}"$ mortises in the back sides of the pieces (four locations for each divider). These will accept the drawer runner tenons. After the milling is completed, apply glue to the dovetailed ends as well as the half-lap opening, and slide the drawer dividers into place.

18 At this time add the contrasting hardwood square pegs by drilling a $\frac{1}{4}"$ hole through the divider and into the center partition, and install a $\frac{1}{4}"$ square peg.

20 Cut the case feet from a rectangular piece sized according to the plan, and save the cutoff. Smooth the cut side and install the foot as shown. Use the waste piece in the gluing process. Also attach a screw through the case bottom and into the foot to add stability and strength. Cut a matching plug from the hardwood selected to fill in the screw-hole area.

19 Cut the drawer runners to size and create the $\frac{1}{2}"$ tenon on one end of the long runners. Apply glue into the mortise and onto the tenon, then install the runner. Finish this step by nailing into the center stile as well as the back stile of each case side and the center partition with a $1\frac{1}{2}"$ nail. The shorter runners (see step 25) are used as top drawer kickers and are nailed at each end at the front of the case.

21 Cut a slot into the case side to receive the clips that will attach the top. I chose to cut a slot as opposed to a continuous groove so as not to weaken the side. My tool of choice is the biscuit joiner. Set the cut for a $\frac{3}{4}"$-deep No. 20 biscuit, and make the first of two cuts for each clip location. Readjust for a $\frac{1}{4}"$ opening and make the second cut. I cut two slots in each side, two in the center partition and four across the front.

22 Build the drawers. (See "Drawer Basics: Hand-cut Dovetails" on page 8.)

23 Using the $\frac{1}{8}$"-radius portion of a cove-and-bead router bit, ease the edge of the countertop.

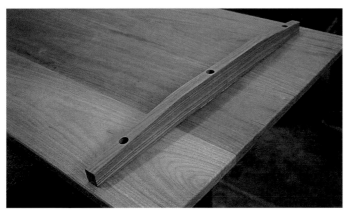

24 Bevel the top supports to 1", starting approximately 7" from each end. From the bottom, counterbore a $\frac{5}{8}$" hole leaving $\frac{3}{4}$" of hardwood in three places (in the middle and 3" from each end). Using a No. 8 × 1$\frac{1}{4}$" screw with a washer in each hole and glue in the center area only, attach the supports to the top just outside the case side.

25 With the case and top inverted, install the clips into the slots and attach to the top with No. 8 × 1$\frac{1}{4}$" screws. Using the same size screws, attach the top to the rear case rail. Sand all parts to 180 grit. Knock off any sharp corners with 120-grit sandpaper and apply a selected finish.

26 The knobs I chose for this counter include four 1$\frac{1}{4}$" knobs for the top two drawers and 12 2"-diameter wooden knobs for all the others. They are ebonized with two coats of water-soluble black aniline dye stain, then finished with sprayed lacquer. Drill holes into the drawer fronts and glue in the knobs.

27 Cut a $\frac{1}{4}$" tongue-and-groove joint on the back pieces. Here I allow three of the pieces to act as legs, one at each end and one at the center of the case, extending an additional 4" and angled to match the front feet.

queen anne
DROP-LEAF
DINING TABLE

WHEN I WAS SELECTING PIECES TO INCLUDE IN THIS BOOK, I felt a dining table was a necessity. This table is based on a number of New England designs from the latter half of the 18th century. It shares characteristics with many drop-leaf tables.

While the tabletop is just 42", it can be used as a small dining table, a breakfast table or as a table behind a sofa. Also, this table can be easily customized to your specific needs by changing minor aspects of the piece, such as the size or shape of the tabletop, or by using a slipper or trifid design for the foot.

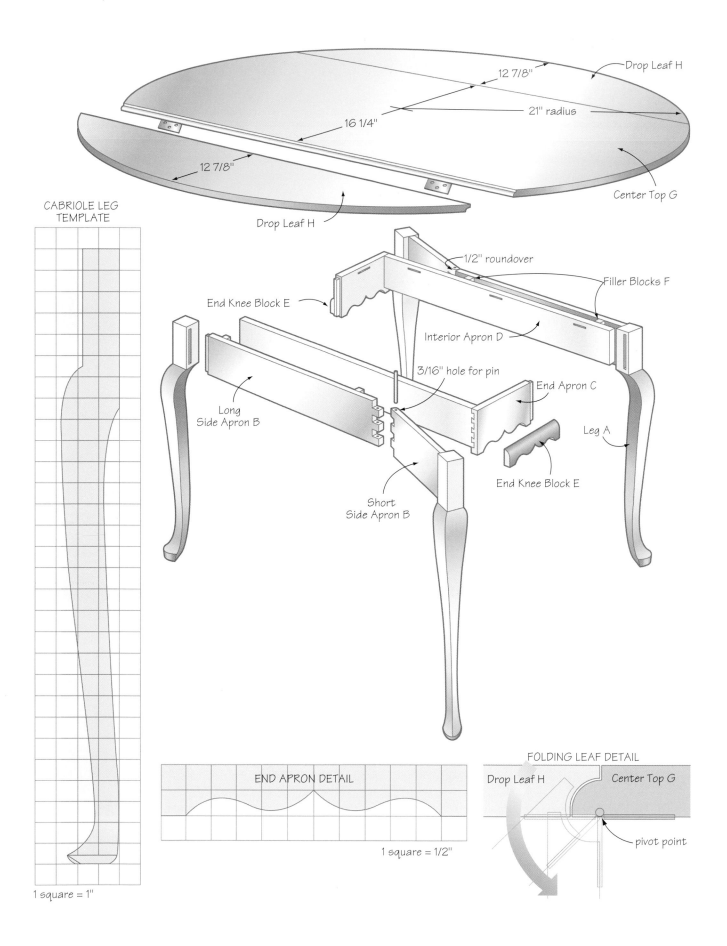

Drop Leaf H

12 7/8"

21" radius

16 1/4"

12 7/8"

Center Top G

Drop Leaf H

CABRIOLE LEG
TEMPLATE

1/2" roundover

Filler Blocks F

End Knee Block E

Interior Apron D

3/16" hole for pin

End Apron C

Long
Side Apron B

Leg A

End Knee Block E

Short
Side Apron B

1 square = 1"

END APRON DETAIL

1 square = 1/2"

FOLDING LEAF DETAIL

Drop Leaf H

Center Top G

pivot point

cutting list | inches

QUEEN ANNE DROP-LEAF TABLE

REFERENCE	QUANTITY	PART	STOCK	THICKNESS	WIDTH	LENGTH	COMMENTS
A	4	Legs	P	$2^3/_4$	$2^3/_4$	29	
B	2	Side Aprons	P	$^{13}/_{16}$	$5^1/_2$	$28^1/_2$	$^3/_4$" TBE rough-cut 4" to 6" longer for hinge joint
C	2	End Aprons	P	$^{13}/_{16}$	$5^1/_2$	$9^3/_4$	$^3/_4$" TOE
D	2	Interior Aprons	P	$^{13}/_{16}$	$5^1/_2$	$27^1/_4$	dovetailed to one end apron
E	2	End Knee Blocks	P	1	$1^3/_4$	9	
F	4	Filler Blocks	S	$^7/_8$	$1^1/_2$	$5^1/_2$	

TABLETOP

REFERENCE	QUANTITY	PART	STOCK	THICKNESS	WIDTH	LENGTH	COMMENTS
G	1	Center Top	P	$^7/_8$	$16^1/_4$	42	
H	2	Drop Leaves	P	$^7/_8$	$12^7/_8$	42	

hardware and supplies

Drop-leaf hinges	2 prs.
Slot-head wood screws	No. 8 × $1^1/_4$"
$^3/_{16}$" Steel rod	12"

cutting list | millimeters

QUEEN ANNE DROP-LEAF TABLE

REFERENCE	QUANTITY	PART	STOCK	THICKNESS	WIDTH	LENGTH	COMMENTS
A	4	Legs	P	70	70	737	
B	2	Side Aprons	P	21	140	724	19mm TBE rough-cut 102mm to 152mm longer for hinge joint
C	2	End Aprons	P	21	140	242	19mm TOE
D	2	Interior Aprons	P	21	140	692	dovetailed to one end apron
E	2	End Knee Blocks	P	25	45	229	
F	4	Filler Blocks	S	22	38	140	

TABLETOP

REFERENCE	QUANTITY	PART	STOCK	THICKNESS	WIDTH	LENGTH	COMMENTS
G	1	Center Top	P	22	412	1067	
H	2	Drop Leaves	P	22	327	1067	

hardware and supplies

Drop-leaf hinges	2 prs.
Slot-head wood screws	No. 8 × 32mm
5mm Steel rod	305mm

TBE = Tenon Both Ends

TOE = Tenon One End

P = Primary Wood

S = Secondary Wood

1 Begin by making the cabriole legs as shown in "Shaping the Cabriole Legs" on page 53.

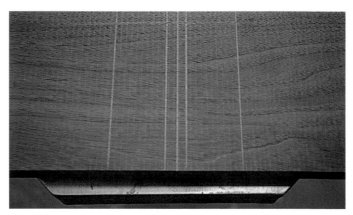

2 Once the legs are shaped, lay out and cut the mortises according to the plan. Begin the process of making the hinged aprons. Make the long aprons with an additional 4" to 6" of length, then move approximately 11" from one end and lay out a centerline. Draw a second set of lines $\frac{1}{4}$" from the centerline. This leaves enough space to cut apart the two long aprons. Finally, draw a third set of lines 2" from the second set. This defines the fingers for your joint.

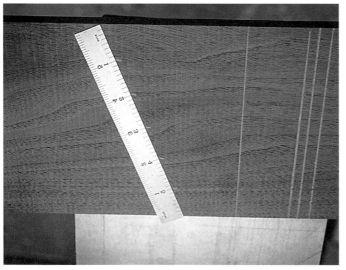

3 Lay out the apron into six equal parts on each side of the group of lines. This is accomplished by setting a rule on an angle at 0" and 6" and marking each inch location.

4 Connect the layout marks to define the individual fingers. Mark an X in the first, third and fifth fingers on one set and the second, fourth and sixth fingers on the opposite set.

5 Set the blade to the correct height and use a miter gauge to remove the X material. Be sure to stay inside the finger lines at each finger. Begin with the longer section of the aprons.

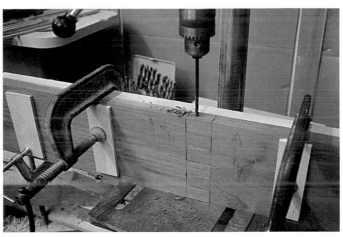

6   Before you cut the short section of the apron, use a $\frac{1}{2}$" roundover bit on the end. Remove the back side of the apron. Here I have marked the finger lines on the back for clarity. Then remove the areas as you did on the longer rail.

7   After you have fine-tuned the fit of the fingers, clamp the assembly to a straightedge placed vertically under the drill press, and drill a $\frac{3}{16}$" hole completely through the fingers. This allows you to install a steel rod to act as a pivot.

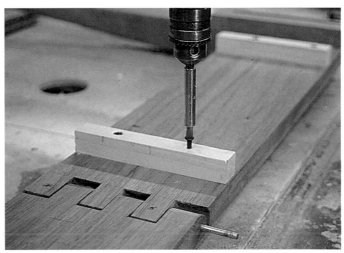

8   With the hinged joint completed, measure and mark $8\frac{7}{8}$" from the joint to the end on the short section and $19\frac{5}{8}$" on the long section. This is the cutoff of the aprons and where the tenons will be cut to match the mortises on the legs. While the apron is apart, remove enough of the bottom of each slot on the fixed apron to allow the square edge of the swing apron to operate.

9   Lay the long apron assembly on the table, inside up, and install the filler blocks as shown using No. 8 × 1$\frac{1}{4}$" wood screws.

10   Mill the interior and end aprons to size. Cut the dovetail joint and the matching tenon for the leg mortises. Rough out the profile for the end apron and knee block. I used a secondary wood, but suggest you use all primary wood because the interior apron shows when the swing leg is opened.

11 Lay the dovetailed portion of the apron onto the inside of the hinged aprons so that the exterior edge of the end apron aligns with the leg block. Attach into the filler blocks as shown using wood screws.

12 Repeat the process on the second set so you have a pair of identical apron assemblies. Before moving on, this is the time to use the biscuit joiner to cut the slots that will receive the wooden clips. (See "Wood Clips" on page 9.)

13 Complete the base of the table by simply sliding the end apron tenons into the leg mortises. If all works well, glue the mortise-and-tenon joints and allow to dry.

14 This is how your completed base should look and operate.

15 With the swing leg firmly clamped to the balance of the base, fit the knee blocks into place and mark the profile that matches each leg on either end of the block.

16 Shape the profile with planes and/or rasps.

17 After you've completed the shaping, mark the knee block decorative pattern onto the block and make the cutout.

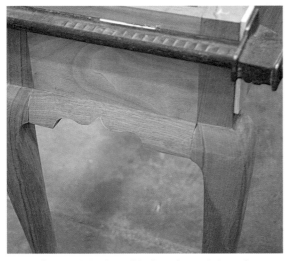

19 Mill the tabletop pieces to size. It is important to keep the sizes correct to fit with the base as you build it. Cut the center top to exact dimensions. Create the rule joint profiles as shown here using a ½" roundover bit on both of the center tabletop edges and a ½" cove bit on one edge of each drop leaf.

18 Reinstall the knee block and attach it to the apron with glue and screws. Be sure no glue gets on the swing leg area.

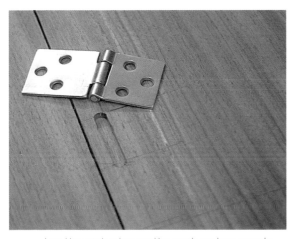

20 Lay the center top on the work surface upside down, then determine the hinge location. Mark a line that is ½" from the edge and create a groove using a ⅜" straight bit directly over that line. This groove is for the barrel of the drop-leaf hinges.

21 Slide the table leaf into place and lay out the hinge, allowing the longer hinge leaf to extend onto the tabletop leaf. Mark the hinge leaves, and create the mortise so the hinge is flush with the bottom of the table when completed.

22 Check the fit of the tabletop by setting it on the base. This is the place to stop if you would like to have a square table; simply rout your edge treatment. However, I chose to create a round top.

23 To achieve a round top, lay the assembled top inverted on the work surface and locate the center. Using a router compass jig (mine was shop-made) set to the correct size and a plunge router with a straight or up-cut straight bit, rout the round shape from the square top.

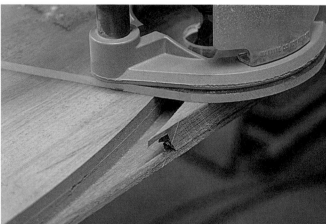

24 Make the cut in multiple passes, then create the desired edge treatment. I simply knocked off the sharp edge with sandpaper, then final sanded.

25 This piece was finished with multiple coats of an oil/varnish mix and wax. (See "Oil/Varnish Finishing" on page 40.) After the finish has been applied, attach the top to the base with the wooden clips.

shaping the cabriole legs

1

After milling your lumber to size, mark the centers on both ends of your stock, and lay out the pattern for the leg onto the stock with the rear leg post areas meeting at one corner. (You will achieve the best look if you orient the grain of the leg to run from that corner toward the knee.) Then using the band saw, cut one side profile carefully. Save the waste pieces. Do not cut the leg post block.

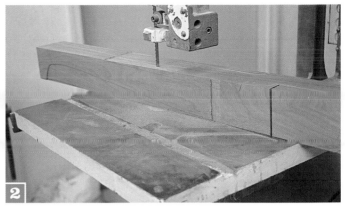

2

Reattach the waste pieces back into the positions from which they came. I like to use a hot-glue gun for this purpose. It dries in a hurry and also acts as a gap filler to replace the band-saw blade thickness. Cut the leg profile on the remaining side. Remove all of the waste material.

3

If you are profiling a Dutch or pad foot, your next step is to turn the foot on the lathe. Mount the blank into position. Check the rotation of the leg prior to turning on the machine. Then use the lathe tools to turn the appropriate shape on the foot as well as on the pad area. If you choose a slipper, trifid or other foot profile, skip this step.

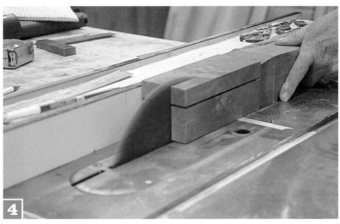

4

Using a saw, raise the blade to the correct height, and mark the front edge of the blade. I use masking tape for this purpose. Then set the fence to just remove the waste of the leg post block and cut to the beginning of the knee profile. Turn the leg a quarter turn and repeat the process. Finish the removal with a handsaw or on the band saw.

5

Shape the leg with a combination of rasps, planes and rifflers to the profile desired (just off-square at the knee to almost completely round at the ankle).

Use common chalk to mark problem areas and finish the shaping with cabinet scrapers until all of the legs are visually identical.

6

townsend newport HIGH CHEST

THE FIRST NAMES THAT COME TO MY MIND WHEN A HIGH chest of drawers (or a "highboy" as it's called today) is mentioned are Goddard and Townsend of Newport, Rhode Island. They developed a style that remained consistent over the years and throughout their large body of work.

I fashioned this highboy based on a piece designed by Christopher Townsend. Built in 1748, with a highly shaped skirt and slipper feet, it is an example of a typical Newport flattop.

If imitation is the sincerest form of flattery, we should all flatter the Townsends by making this piece.

FROM THE COLLECTION OF RICHARD AND ELIZABETH WILLIAMS, WILLIAMSTOWN, MASSACHUSETTS

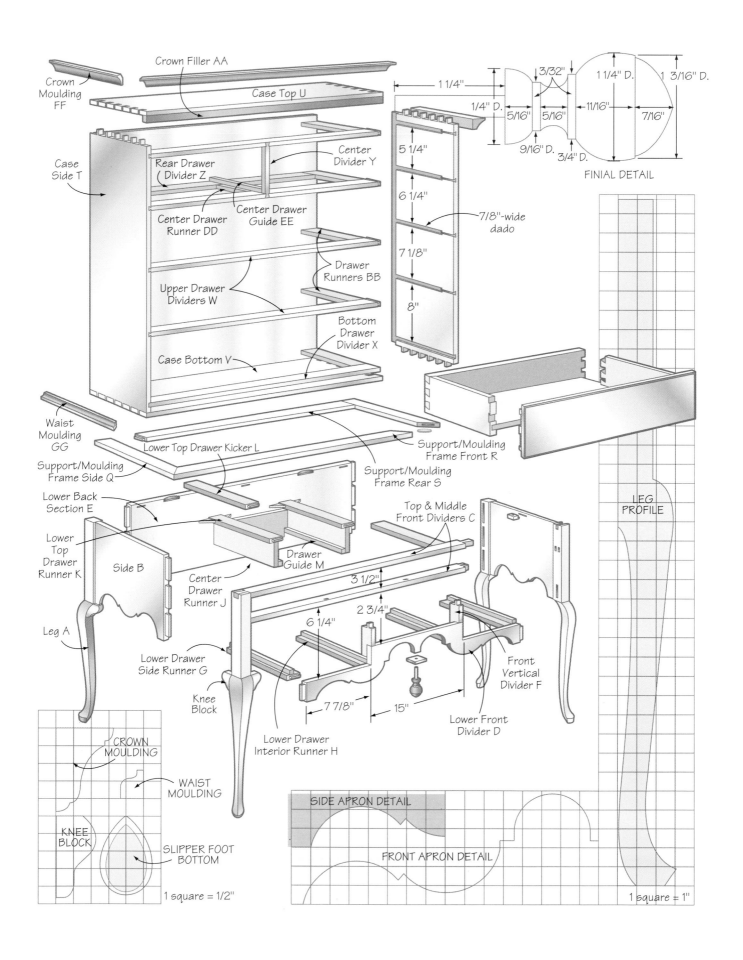

Crown Moulding FF

Crown Filler AA

Case Top U

1 1/4"

3/32"

1 1/4" D.

1 3/16" D.

1/4" D.

5/16" 5/16"

11/16"

7/16"

9/16" D.

3/4" D.

FINIAL DETAIL

Case Side T

Rear Drawer Divider Z

Center Divider Y

5 1/4"

Center Drawer Runner DD

Center Drawer Guide EE

6 1/4"

7/8"-wide dado

Upper Drawer Dividers W

7 1/8"

Drawer Runners BB

8"

Bottom Drawer Divider X

Case Bottom V

Waist Moulding GG

Lower Top Drawer Kicker L

Support/Moulding Frame Front R

Support/Moulding Frame Side Q

Support/Moulding Frame Rear S

LEG PROFILE

Lower Back Section E

Top & Middle Front Dividers C

Lower Top Drawer Runner K

Side B

Drawer Guide M

Center Drawer Runner J

3 1/2"

2 3/4"

Leg A

Lower Drawer Side Runner G

6 1/4"

Front Vertical Divider F

Knee Block

Lower Drawer Interior Runner H

7 7/8"

15"

Lower Front Divider D

CROWN MOULDING

WAIST MOULDING

KNEE BLOCK

SLIPPER FOOT BOTTOM

1 square = 1/2"

SIDE APRON DETAIL

FRONT APRON DETAIL

1 square = 1"

cutting list | inches

TOWNSEND NEWPORT HIGH CHEST

LOWER SECTION OF HIGH CHEST OF DRAWERS

REFERENCE	QUANTITY	PART	STOCK	THICKNESS	WIDTH	LENGTH	COMMENTS
A	4	Legs	P	3	3	$35^3/4$	
B	2	Sides	P	$3/4$	$14^1/2$	$18^1/8$	1" TBE
C	2	Top and Middle Front Dividers	P	$3/4$	$1^5/8$	35	1" TBE
D	1	Lower Front Divider	P	$3/4$	7	35	1" TBE
E	1	Lower Section Back	S	$3/4$	$14^1/2$	35	1" TBE
F	2	Front Vertical Dividers	P	$1^1/8$	$1^5/8$	$7^1/8$	$3/4$" TOE
G	2	Lower Drawer Side Runners	P	$3/4$	$1^5/8$	$17^1/2$	$7/8$" notch for legs
H	2	Lower Drawer Interior Runners	P	$3/4$	2	$17^1/2$	$3/8$" TOE
J	2	Center Dwr. Runners	P	$3/4$	2	$16^5/8$	$3/8$" TOE
K	2	Lower Top Drawer Runners	P	$3/4$	2	$16^5/8$	$3/8$" TOE, notch for leg
L	2	Lower Top Drawer Kickers	P	$3/4$	2	$17^1/2$	$3/8$" × $3/8$" rabbet at back
M	6	Drawer Guides	S	$5/8$	$5/8$	$15^5/8$	
N	3	Small Center Drawer Hangers	S	$5/8$	$3^1/2$	15	
P	2	Small Center Drawer Runners	S	$9/16$	$9/16$	$15^1/8$	
Q	2	Support/Moulding Frame Sides	P	$3/4$	$3^1/2$	$19^1/2$	45° OE; mortise OE
R	1	Support/Moulding Frame Front	P	$3/4$	$3^1/2$	$37^1/4$	45° BE
S	1	Support/Moulding Frame Rear	S	$3/4$	$3^1/2$	$32^1/4$	1" TBE

UPPER SECTION OF HIGH CHEST OF DRAWERS

REFERENCE	QUANTITY	PART	STOCK	THICKNESS	WIDTH	LENGTH	COMMENTS
T	2	Case Sides	P	$7/8$	$18^1/8$	$33^3/4$	
U	1	Case Top	P	$3/4$	$18^1/8$	$34^1/2$	
V	1	Case Bottom	S	$5/8$	$18^1/8$	$34^1/2$	
W	4	Upper Drawer Dividers	P	$7/8$	2	$33^3/4$	dovetailed ends
X	1	Bottom Drawer Divider	P	$7/8$	2	$32^3/4$	not dovetailed
Y	1	Center Divider	P	$7/8$	1	7	dovetailed ends
Z	1	Rear Drawer Divider	S	$7/8$	2	$33^3/8$	
AA	1	Crown Filler	S	$3/4$	$1^3/8$	$32^3/4$	
BB	8	Drawer Runners	S	$7/8$	1	$15^3/4$	$3/8$" TOE
CC	2	Drawer Runners for Split Drawers	S	$7/8$	1	$14^3/4$	$3/8$" TOE; 1" TOE
DD	1	Center Drawer Runner	S	$7/8$	3	$14^3/4$	$3/8$" TOE; 1" TOE
EE	1	Center Drawer Guide	S	$3/4$	1	$14^3/4$	
FF	2	Crown Moulding	P	$1^5/8$	$2^3/8$	45	
GG	2	Waist Moulding	P	$3/4$	$3/4$	42	

DRAWER PARTS

REFERENCE	QUANTITY	PART	STOCK	THICKNESS	WIDTH	LENGTH	COMMENTS
HH	2	Drawer Fronts	P	$7/8$	$6^1/2$	$8^1/2$	$3/8$" lip, three sides
JJ	1	Drawer Front	P	$7/8$	3	$15^5/8$	
KK	1	Drawer Front	P	$7/8$	$3^3/4$	$33^5/8$	
LL	2	Drawer Fronts	P	$7/8$	$5^1/2$	$16^9/16$	
MM	1	Drawer Front	P	$7/8$	$6^1/2$	$33^1/2$	
NN	1	Drawer Front	P	$7/8$	$7^3/8$	$33^1/2$	
PP	1	Drawer Front	P	$7/8$	$8^1/4$	$33^1/2$	
QQ	4	Drawer Sides	S	$1/2$	$5^1/8$	16	
RR	6	Drawer Sides	S	$1/2$	$6^1/8$	16	
SS	2	Drawer Sides	S	$1/2$	7	16	
TT	2	Drawer Sides	S	$1/2$	$7^7/8$	16	
UU	2	Drawer Sides	S	$1/2$	$3^1/8$	16	
VV	2	Drawer Sides	S	$1/2$	$2^5/8$	16	
WW	2	Drawer Sides	S	$1/2$	$5^3/8$	$7^3/4$	
XX	1	Drawer Back	S	$1/2$	$1^7/8$	$14^7/8$	
YY	1	Drawer Back	S	$1/2$	$2^3/8$	$32^7/8$	
ZZ	2	Drawer Back	S	$1/2$	$4^3/8$	$15^3/4$	
AAA	1	Drawer Back	S	$1/2$	$5^3/8$	$32^3/4$	
BBB	1	Drawer Back	S	$1/2$	$6^1/4$	$32^3/4$	
CCC	1	Drawer Back	S	$1/2$	$7^1/8$	$32^3/4$	
DDD	2	Drawer Bottoms	S	$5/8$	$16^1/4$	$15^1/4$	
EEE	3	Drawer Bottoms	S	$5/8$	$16^1/4$	$32^1/8$	
FFF	1	Drawer Bottom	S	$5/8$	$16^1/4$	$32^3/8$	
GGG	2	Drawer Bottoms	S	$5/8$	$16^1/4$	$7^1/8$	
HHH	1	Drawer Bottom	S	$5/8$	$16^1/4$	$14^7/16$	
JJJ	1	Backboards	S	$5/8$	$33^{11}/16$	$32^3/8$	many pieces

TBE = Tenon Both Ends

TOE = Tenon One End

P = Primary Wood

S = Secondary Wood

hardware and supplies

HORTON BRASSES HARDWARE:

Chippendale pulls	6, size H-15, antique finish
Chippendale pulls	1, size H-15S, antique finish
Matching escutcheons	4, size H-15SE, antique finish

cutting list | millimeters

TOWNSEND NEWPORT HIGH CHEST

LOWER SECTION OF HIGH CHEST OF DRAWERS

REFERENCE	QUANTITY	PART	STOCK	THICKNESS	WIDTH	LENGTH	COMMENTS
A	4	Legs	P	76	76	908	
B	2	Sides	P	19	369	460	25mm TBE
C	2	Top and Middle Front Dividers	P	19	41	889	25mm TBE
D	1	Lower Front Divider	P	19	178	889	25mm TBE
E	1	Lower Section Back	S	19	369	889	25mm TBE
F	2	Front Vertical Dividers	P	29	41	181	19mm TOE
G	2	Lower Drawer Side Runners	P	19	41	445	22mm notch for legs
H	2	Lower Drawer Interior Runners	P	19	51	445	10mm TOE
J	2	Center Dwr. Runners	P	19	51	445	10mm TOE
K	2	Lower Top Drawer Runners	P	19	51	422	10mm TOE notch for leg
L	2	Lower Top Dwr. Kickers	P	19	51	445	10mm × 10mm rabbet at back
M	6	Drawer Guides	S	16	16	397	
N	3	Small Center Drawer Hangers	S	16	89	381	
P	2	Small Center Drawer Runners	S	14	14	384	
Q	2	Support/Moulding Frame Sides	P	19	89	496	45° OE; mortise OE
R	1	Support/Moulding Frame Front	P	19	89	946	45° BE
S	1	Support/Moulding Frame Rear	S	19	89	819	25mm TBE

UPPER SECTION OF HIGH CHEST OF DRAWERS

REFERENCE	QUANTITY	PART	STOCK	THICKNESS	WIDTH	LENGTH	COMMENTS
T	2	Case Sides	P	22	460	857	
U	1	Case Top	P	19	460	877	
V	1	Case Bottom	S	16	460	877	
W	4	Upper Drawer Dividers	P	22	51	857	dovetailed ends
X	1	Bottom Drawer Divider	P	22	51	832	not dovetailed
Y	1	Center Divider	P	22	25	178	dovetailed ends
Z	1	Rear Drawer Divider	S	22	51	848	
AA	1	Crown Filler	S	19	35	832	
BB	8	Drawer Runners	S	22	25	400	10mm TOE
CC	2	Drawer Runners for Split Drawers	S	22	25	375	10mm TOE; 25mm TOE
DD	1	Center Drawer Runner	S	22	76	375	10mm TOE; 25mm TOE
EE	1	Center Drawer Guide	S	19	25	375	
FF	2	Crown Moulding	P	41	61	1143	
GG	2	Waist Moulding	P	19	19	1067	

DRAWER PARTS

REFERENCE	QUANTITY	PART	STOCK	THICKNESS	WIDTH	LENGTH	COMMENTS
HH	2	Drawer Fronts	P	22	165	216	10mm lip three sides
JJ	1	Drawer Front	P	22	76	397	
KK	1	Drawer Front	P	22	95	854	
LL	2	Drawer Fronts	P	22	140	420	
MM	1	Drawer Front	P	22	165	851	
NN	1	Drawer Front	P	22	188	851	
PP	1	Drawer Front	P	22	209	851	
QQ	4	Drawer Sides	S	13	130	406	
RR	6	Drawer Sides	S	13	155	406	
SS	2	Drawer Sides	S	13	178	406	
TT	2	Drawer Sides	S	13	200	406	
UU	2	Drawer Sides	S	13	79	406	
VV	2	Drawer Sides	S	13	67	406	
WW	2	Drawer Sides	S	13	137	197	
XX	1	Drawer Back	S	13	47	378	
YY	1	Drawer Back	S	13	61	835	
ZZ	2	Drawer Backs	S	13	112	400	
AAA	1	Drawer Back	S	13	137	832	
BBB	1	Drawer Back	S	13	158	832	
CCC	1	Drawer Back	S	13	181	832	
DDD	2	Drawer Bottoms	S	16	412	387	
EEE	3	Drawer Bottoms	S	16	412	816	
FFF	1	Drawer Bottom	S	16	412	823	
GGG	2	Drawer Bottoms	S	16	412	181	
HHH	1	Drawer Bottoms	S	16	412	367	
JJJ	1	Backboards	S	16	856	823	many pieces

TBE = Tenon Both Ends

TOE = Tenon One End

P = Primary Wood

S = Secondary Wood

hardware and supplies

HORTON BRASSES HARDWARE:

Chippendale pulls	6, size H-15, antique finish	
Chippendale pulls	1, size H-15S, antique finish	
Matching escutcheons	4, size H-15SE, antique finish	

1 Begin with the cabriole legs (see "Shaping the Cabriole Legs" on page 53). After shaping the legs to the foot, position the egg-shaped pattern to create the slipper foot. Use a coping saw to cut on an angle from the bottom or inside of the shape to the top or outer marking on the pattern. This creates a slight bevel on the foot from top to bottom.

2 Lay out and cut the mortises for the front rails, sides and back.

3 The front top rail is dovetailed into the top of the front legs. Lay out the tail and remove as much as possible with a flat-bottom drill bit. Then clean up the joint with chisels.

4 This is the layout of the front legs for the front rails. Notice that the center rail is a double tenon cut. You also can see the finished dovetail cut for the top rail.

Tip On all highly figured woods, or if your cutter is not as sharp as it should be, it helps tremendously to wet the edges of the panels before cutting the raised panel design. Just remember to fit the panel on the end grain because the wetting will temporarily expand the wood.

5 Mill all the required pieces for the lower case, and cut the matching tenons. This is how the side and back tenons look. Don't forget to cut the mortises in the front rails for the drawer runners.

6 Temporarily install the front lower rails; then by setting the inverted assembly onto the top rail, you can mark and cut the dovetail to fit the opening.

7 Place the profile for the sides and the front in position on the appropriate stock, then mark and cut your pieces. After cutting the profile onto the front lower rail, cut the waste at the drawer front.

8 Cut and install the center drawer vertical dividers. They mortise into the middle rail and lap behind the lower front rail. Attach them with glue and two No. 8 × 1¹⁄₄" wood screws.

Tip If you are milling a board wider than your jointer, mill as much surface as you can, then place the flat side onto a sled of plywood of a size equal to your jointer cut, and run the piece through the planer. With one side completely flat, finish the process in the usual manner.

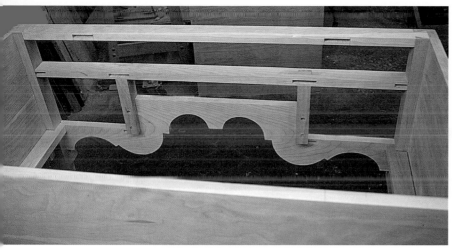

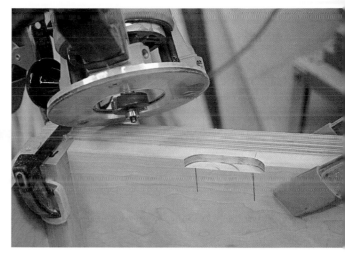

9 This is a view of the front of the piece from the inside. Make sure you have all the mortises, then assemble the lower section.

10 Use a router and a rabbet bit to cut the waste from the back to house the drawer kicker. Then cut the slots for the wooden clips used to attach the frame. (See step 21 on page 42.)

11 Install the lower top drawer runners using a bridle joint at the rear of the case. Glue the side runners into the mortises in the front, then nail the runners into the rear leg posts.

12 Construct the dovetailed U-shape section for the small central drawer. Attach it with screws and glue to the underside of the kickers that work with the lower side drawers (it actually hangs from the underside). Then finish installing the runners for the small central drawer. Use a small glue block at the front and make sure the edge of the section is flush with the face frame; it will act as the drawer guide.

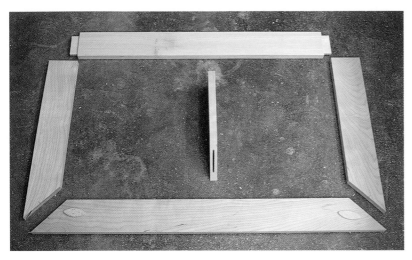

13 Mill the pieces for the frame that attaches to the top of the lower section. Cut the angle cuts at the front of both sides and on both ends of the front, and create the biscuit joint in each. Then make the mortises in the rear of each side and tenons to match in the back piece. Then glue the frame, rout the profile when dry, and install with the clips to the top of the base. (See "Wood Clips" on page 9.)

14 Time to make the knee blocks. The most important step is to match the grain of the block to the legs. Here you see the evolution of a knee block. Take a square block, set it against the leg and trace the profile. Cut the square to that design, apply the pattern and, finally, cut to the pattern profile.

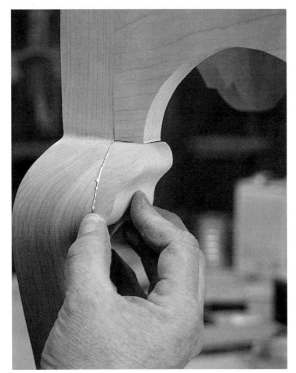

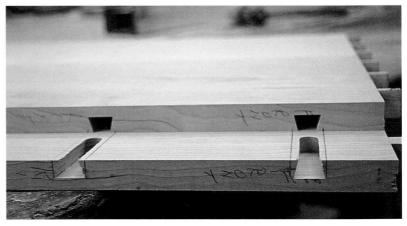

16 Now for the upper section. Mill and cut to size the sides, top and bottom. Then dovetail the case with tails in the sides and the pins at top and bottom. Lay out and cut the dovetail slots for the drawer dividers.

15 Attach the knee block and, when dry, use files and chisels to trim to a smooth transition from the leg.

17 Square a line to the back of the case drawn from the dovetail slots. This is to create a shouldered half-blind dovetail joint for the rail, as well as to support the runners.

19 Cut and install the dovetails for the top drawer vertical divider and, using a piece of scrap, fill in the area above the first divider and the top of the case. This eventually will be covered with the crown moulding.

18 Cut the dovetail ends on the dividers and mortise the backs for the runner tenons. Then install the dividers into the case.

20 Affix the drawer runner tenons into the mortises in the front dividers, and nail into the case sides at the rear. Notice that the runners for the top drawers are mortised into the rear divider, which houses the side runners and the center runner. This rear divider is nailed from the bottom through the divider into the case side at a slight angle.

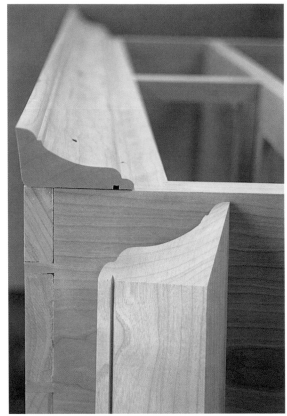

21 Final sand the case to 180 grit, then create the crown moulding according to the profile and install with glue and nails. Notice the small groove made on the table saw; it allows excess glue to be captured in the slot instead of spreading onto the front surface.

22 Set the upper section onto the lower section and cut the intermediate waist moulding. Install the moulding by nailing it into the lower section frame. Leave a bit of room at the back to allow the upper section to slide into the moulded area. I use a piece of sanding disc as a spacer.

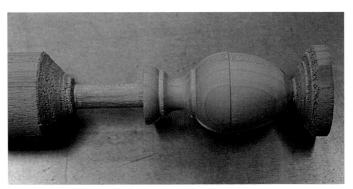

23 Create the beaded platform from which the finial will protrude by cutting a block to size, moulding the bottom edge with a beading bit, then slicing the piece from the block.

24 Turn the finial, which is an acorn in design.

25 With the lower section inverted, drill a hole to receive the finial. To help drill a straight hole, I drill through a square block and hold that block onto the flat surface of the lower apron.

26 Referring to the plan, build the drawers to the necessary sizes. (See "Drawer Basics: Handcut Dovetails" on page 8.)

27 Make the half-lap pieces for the backboards, then final sand all pieces for finishing.

28 Apply the finish. I chose to use buttonlac shellac. Spray two to three coats; be sure to sand between each coat! Then glaze and spray two additional coats of shellac. Sand and apply one coat of dull-rubbed-effect lacquer. Install the hardware.

new york/canadian STEPBACK

THE ANTIQUE ON WHICH I BASED THIS DESIGN IS OWNED BY A friend of mine. I first saw it many years ago and immediately was captured by the boldness of the five-step crown and the raised-panel sides. Add to that a row of drawers located in the upper section, and you have a cupboard that definitely demands attention.

While the antique version featured original paint and I chose to paint this modern version, it also would look great stained in tiger maple or cherry hues.

Looking at the construction methods employed, it becomes obvious that the original version of this cupboard was produced by a country craftsman — a craftsman with a very good eye for proportion and detail.

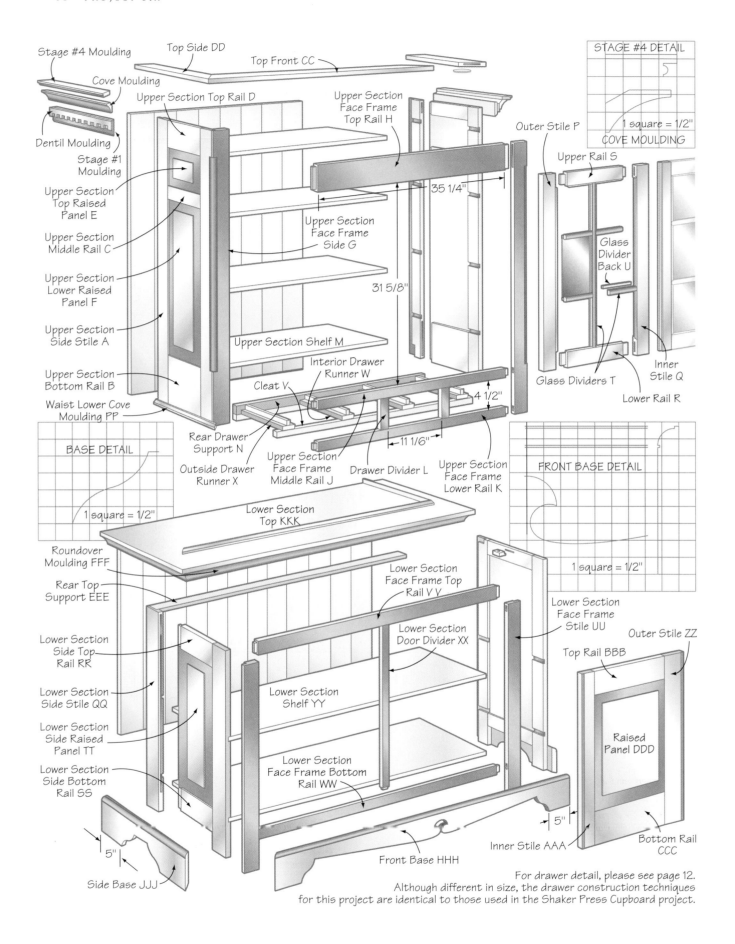

Stage #4 Moulding

Top Side DD

Top Front CC

Cove Moulding

Upper Section Top Rail D

Upper Section Face Frame Top Rail H

STAGE #4 DETAIL

Dentil Moulding

1 square = 1/2"

COVE MOULDING

Stage #1 Moulding

Outer Stile P

Upper Rail S

Upper Section Top Raised Panel E

Upper Section Middle Rail C

Upper Section Face Frame Side G

35 1/4"

Glass Divider Back U

Upper Section Lower Raised Panel F

31 5/8"

Upper Section Side Stile A

Upper Section Shelf M

Glass Dividers T

Inner Stile Q

Upper Section Bottom Rail B

Interior Drawer Runner W

Lower Rail R

Waist Lower Cove Moulding PP

Cleat V

4 1/2"

BASE DETAIL

Rear Drawer Support N

Upper Section Face Frame Middle Rail J

Drawer Divider L

Upper Section Face Frame Lower Rail K

11 1/6"

FRONT BASE DETAIL

Outside Drawer Runner X

1 square = 1/2"

Lower Section Top KKK

1 square = 1/2"

Roundover Moulding FFF

Lower Section Face Frame Top Rail V V

Rear Top Support EEE

Lower Section Face Frame Stile UU

Outer Stile ZZ

Lower Section Side Top Rail RR

Lower Section Door Divider XX

Top Rail BBB

Lower Section Side Stile QQ

Lower Section Shelf YY

Lower Section Side Raised Panel TT

Raised Panel DDD

Lower Section Face Frame Bottom Rail WW

Lower Section Side Bottom Rail SS

5"

Inner Stile AAA

Bottom Rail CCC

5"

Front Base HHH

Side Base JJJ

For drawer detail, please see page 12. Although different in size, the drawer construction techniques for this project are identical to those used in the Shaker Press Cupboard project.

cutting list | inches

NEW YORK/CANADIAN STEPBACK

UPPER SECTION

REFERENCE	QUANTITY	PART	STOCK	THICKNESS	WIDTH	LENGTH	
A	4	Side Stiles	P	$7/8$	3	45	
B	2	Bottom Rails	P	$7/8$	$7^5/8$	9	$1^1/4$" TBE
C	2	Middle Rails	P	$7/8$	$2^3/4$	9	$1^1/4$" TBE
D	2	Top Rails	P	$7/8$	$5^3/4$	9	$1^1/4$" TBE
E	2	Top Raised Panels	P	$5/8$	$7^1/8$	$7^1/8$	
F	2	Lower Raised Panels	P	$5/8$	$7^1/8$	23	
G	2	Face-Frame Sides	P	$7/8$	$3^5/8$	45	
H	1	Face-Frame Top Rail	P	$7/8$	$5^3/4$	$37^3/4$	$1^1/4$" TBE
J	1	Face-Frame Middle Rail	P	$7/8$	$1^1/2$	$37^3/4$	$1^1/4$" TBE
K	1	Face-Frame Lower Rail	P	$7/8$	$1^5/8$	$37^3/4$	$1^1/4$" TBE
L	2	Face-Frame Dwr. Dividers	P	$7/8$	1	6	$3/4$" TBE
M	4	Shelves	P	$3/4$	$11^1/2$	$42^1/8$	
N	1	Rear Drawer Support	P	$3/4$	$2^3/4$	$41^9/16$	

LOWER SECTION

REFERENCE	QUANTITY	PART	STOCK	THICKNESS	WIDTH	LENGTH	
QQ	4	Side Stiles		$7/8$	$3^1/2$	34	
RR	2	Side Top Rails		$7/8$	$2^7/8$	$11^1/4$	$1^1/4$" TBE
SS	2	Side Bottom Rails		$7/8$	$3^5/8$	$11^1/4$	$1^1/4$" TBE
TT	2	Side Raised Panels		$5/8$	$9^3/8$	$24^7/8$	TBE
UU	2	Face-Frame Stiles		$7/8$	$4^1/4$	34	
VV	1	Face-Frame Top Rail		$7/8$	$2^7/8$	$42^3/4$	$1/4$" TBE
WW	1	Face-Frame Bottom Rail		$7/8$	$3^5/8$	$42^3/4$	$1/4$" TBE
XX	1	Door Divider		$7/8$	2	$26^7/8$	$1/4$" TBE
YY	2	Shelves		$3/4$	$14^5/8$	$47^5/16$	

UPPER DOORS

REFERENCE	QUANTITY	PART	STOCK	THICKNESS	WIDTH	LENGTH	
P	2	Outer Stiles	P	$7/8$	$1^5/8$	$31^5/8$	
Q	2	Inner Stiles	P	$7/8$	$1^7/8$	$31^5/8$	
R	2	Lower Rails	P	$7/8$	$2^3/8$	$16^1/8$	1" TBE
S	2	Upper Rails	P	$7/8$	2	$16^1/8$	1" TBE
T	4	Moulded Pieces for Glass Dividers	P	$1/4$	$5/8$	30	
U	4	Backs for Glass Dividers	P	$3/16$	$5/8$	30	
V	2	Cleating at Dwr. Area	P	$3/4$	1	$40^9/16$	
W	2	Interior Drawer Runners and Guides	P	$7/8$	$2^1/2$	$10^5/8$	
X	2	Outside Drawer Runners and Guides	P	$7/8$	$1^3/4$	$10^5/8$	

DRAWER PARTS

REFERENCE	QUANTITY	PART	STOCK	THICKNESS	WIDTH	LENGTH
Y	3	Drawer Fronts	P	$7/8$	$4^1/2$	11
Z	6	Drawer Sides	P	$7/16$	$4^1/2$	10
AA	3	Drawer Backs	P	$7/16$	$3^3/4$	11
BB	3	Drawer Bottoms	P	$1/2$	$10^1/4$	$10^1/2$

UPPER SECTION MOULDINGS

REFERENCE	QUANTITY	PART	STOCK	THICKNESS	WIDTH	LENGTH	
CC	1	Top Front	P	$5/8$	$4^7/8$	$50^1/2$	
DD	2	Top Sides	P	$5/8$	$4^7/8$	$17^1/8$	
EE	1	Stage No. 1 Front	P	$1/2$	$1^7/8$	45	between case and dentil
FF	1	Stage No. 1 Side	P	$1/2$	$1^7/8$	30	between case and dentil
GG	1	Dentil Front	P	$3/8$	$1^5/8$	45	
HH	2	Dentil Sides	P	$3/8$	$1^5/8$	15	
JJ	1	Cove Front	P	$3/4$	$2^1/2$	52	
KK	2	Cove Sides	P	$3/4$	$2^1/2$	18	
LL	1	Stage No. 4 Front	P	$5/8$	2	52	
MM	2	Stage No. 4 Sides	P	$5/8$	2	18	
NN	1	Waist Lower Cove Front	P	$7/8$	$7/8$	45	
PP	2	Waist Lower Cove Sides	P	$7/8$	$7/8$	18	

LOWER SECTION MOULDINGS

REFERENCE	QUANTITY	PART	STOCK	THICKNESS	WIDTH	LENGTH	
FFF	1	$1/2$" Roundover Moulding	P	$7/8$	$7/8$	52	below top front
GGG	2	$1/2$" Roundover Moulding	P	$7/8$	$7/8$	18	below top sides
HHH	1	Front Base	P	$5/8$	$4^3/8$	52	
JJJ	2	Side Bases	P	$5/8$	$4^3/8$	18	
KKK	1	Lower Section Top	P	$7/8$	$17^3/4$	$51^3/4$	
LLL	1	Upper Section Backboards	P	$5/8$	$41^3/4$	$44^7/8$	total area
MMM	1	Lower Section Backboards	P	$5/8$	48	29	total area with two end pieces for feet

LOWER DOORS

REFERENCE	QUANTITY	PART	STOCK	THICKNESS	WIDTH	LENGTH	
ZZ	2	Outer Stiles	P	$7/8$	$3^1/4$	$24^3/8$	
AAA	2	Inner Stiles	P	$7/8$	$2^7/8$	$24^3/8$	
BBB	2	Top Rails	P	$7/8$	$2^7/8$	$15^3/8$	$1/4$" TBE
CCC	2	Bottom Rails	P	$7/8$	$4^1/2$	$15^3/8$	$1/4$" TBE
DDD	2	Raised Panels	P	$5/8$	$13^1/2$	$17^5/8$	
EEE	1	Lower Section Rear Top Support	P	$3/4$	$2^1/4$	$46^{15}/16$	

TBE = Tenon Both Ends
P = Primary Wood
S = Secondary Wood

hardware and supplies

Butt hinges	4 prs., $1^1/2$"
Slot-head wood screws	No. 8 x $1^1/4$"

HORTON BRASSES HARDWARE:

K-12 4, $3/4$" with wood screws	antique finish
CP-20 cupboard turn for upper door	antique finish
P-97 cupboard turns for lower doors	2 (with PRT-20L extra-long fingers)
N-7 $1^1/2$" clout or shingle nail	

cutting list | millimeters

NEW YORK/CANADIAN STEPBACK

UPPER SECTION

REFERENCE	QUANTITY	PART	STOCK	THICKNESS	WIDTH	LENGTH	
A	4	Side Stiles	P	22	76	1143	
B	2	Bottom Rails	P	22	194	229	32mm TBE
C	2	Middle Rails	P	22	70	229	32mm TBE
D	2	Top Rails	P	22	146	229	32mm TBE
E	2	Top Raised Panels	P	16	181	181	
F	2	Lower Raised Panels	P	16	181	584	
G	2	Face-Frame Sides	P	22	92	1143	
H	1	Face-Frame Top Rail	P	22	146	959	32mm TBE
J	1	Face-Frame Middle Rail	P	22	38	959	32mm TBE
K	1	Face-Frame Lower Rail	P	22	41	959	32mm TBE
L	2	Face-Frame Dwr. Dividers	P	22	25	152	19mm TBE
M	4	Shelves	P	19	292	1070	
N	1	Rear Drawer Support	P	19	70	1055	

LOWER SECTION

REFERENCE	QUANTITY	PART	STOCK	THICKNESS	WIDTH	LENGTH	
QQ	4	Side Stiles		22	89	864	
RR	2	Side Top Rails		22	73	285	32mm TBE
SS	2	Side Bottom Rails		22	92	285	32mm TBE
TT	2	Side Raised Panels		16	239	632	TBE
UU	2	Face-Frame Stiles		22	210	864	
VV	1	Face-Frame Top Rail		22	73	1086	6mm TBE
WW	1	Face-Frame Bottom Rail		22	92	1086	6mm TBE
XX	1	Door Divider		22	51	682	6mm TBE
YY	2	Shelves		19	372	1218	

UPPER DOORS

REFERENCE	QUANTITY	PART	STOCK	THICKNESS	WIDTH	LENGTH	
P	2	Outer Stiles	P	22	41	803	
Q	2	Inner Stiles	P	22	47	803	
R	2	Lower Rails	P	22	61	409	25mm TBE
S	2	Upper Rails	P	22	51	409	25mm TBE
T	4	Moulded Pieces for Glass Dividers	P	6	16	762	
U	4	Backs for Glass Dividers	P	5	16	762	
V	2	Cleating at Dwr. Area	P	19	25	1030	
W	2	Interior Drawer Runners and Guides	P	22	64	270	
X	2	Outside Drawer Runners and Guides	P	22	45	270	

DRAWER PARTS

REFERENCE	QUANTITY	PART	STOCK	THICKNESS	WIDTH	LENGTH
Y	3	Drawer Fronts	P	22	115	279
Z	6	Drawer Sides	P	11	115	254
AA	3	Drawer Backs	P	11	95	279
BB	3	Drawer Bottoms	P	13	260	267

UPPER SECTION MOULDINGS

REFERENCE	QUANTITY	PART	STOCK	THICKNESS	WIDTH	LENGTH	
CC	1	Top Front	P	16	124	1283	
DD	2	Top Sides	P	16	124	435	
EE	1	Stage No. 1 Front	P	13	47	1143	between case and dentil
FF	1	Stage No. 1 Side	P	13	47	762	between case and dentil
GG	1	Dentil Front	P	10	41	1143	
HH	2	Dentil Sides	P	10	41	381	
JJ	1	Cove Front	P	19	64	1320	
KK	2	Cove Sides	P	19	64	457	
LL	1	Stage No. 4 Front	P	16	51	1320	
MM	2	Stage No. 4 Sides	P	16	51	457	
NN	1	Waist Lower Cove Front	P	22	22	1143	
PP	2	Waist Lower Cove Sides	P	22	22	457	

LOWER SECTION MOULDINGS

REFERENCE	QUANTITY	PART	STOCK	THICKNESS	WIDTH	LENGTH	
FFF	1	13mm Roundover Moulding	P	22	22	1320	below top front
GGG	2	13mm Roundover Moulding	P	22	22	457	below top sides
HHH	1	Front Base	P	16	112	1320	
JJJ	2	Side Bases	P	16	112	457	
KKK	1	Lower Section Top	P	22	451	1314	
LLL	1	Upper Section Backboards	P	16	1060	1140	total area
MMM	1	Lower Section Backboards	P	16	1219	737	total area with two end pieces for feet

LOWER DOORS

REFERENCE	QUANTITY	PART	STOCK	THICKNESS	WIDTH	LENGTH	
ZZ	2	Outer Stiles	P	22	82	620	
AAA	2	Inner Stiles	P	22	73	620	
BBB	2	Top Rails	P	22	73	391	6mm TBE
CCC	2	Bottom Rails	P	22	115	391	6mm TBE
DDD	2	Raised Panels	P	16	343	448	
EEE	1	Lower Section Rear Top Support	P	19	57	1192	

TBE = Tenon Both Ends

P = Primary Wood

S = Secondary Wood

hardware and supplies

Butt Hinges	4 prs., 38mm
Slot-head Wood Screws	No. 8 x 32mm

HORTON BRASSES HARDWARE:

K-12, 4, 19mm with wood screws	Antique finish
CP-20 cupboard turn for upper door	Antique finish
P-97 cupboard turns for lower doors	2 (with PRT-20L extra-long fingers)
N-7 38mm clout or shingle nail	

1 Create the mortise-and-tenon joints for all the pieces of the sides of the lower section.

2 When the joinery is complete, mill the $\frac{1}{4}$" groove to accept the raised panels. If you drop cut the grooves, you will not need to haunch the tenons.

3 Dry fit the side frames and check the measurements for the panels. Don't forget to add the $\frac{5}{8}$" for the recessed portion of the panels. Cut the panels to size and create the raised panel detail with a shaper or panel-raising bit in the router table.

4 After the panels are finished, sand the edges and assemble the sides. Glue the mortise-and-tenon joints, but allow the panels to float. When dry, install the pegs.

5 Locate the bottom and shelf positions and create the $\frac{3}{16}$" × $\frac{3}{4}$" dado in the interior of the sides. The bottom also acts as a doorstop. Then cut the rabbet for the backboards.

6 Using the mortise-and-tenon joint at all intersections, mill and assemble the front face frame. Peg the joints with a $\frac{1}{4}$" peg.

7 The next step is quite different from typical construction methods. Due to the front corner edge treatment of these cases, it is necessary to allow only $\frac{5}{8}$" to extend to the outside edge of the case. So we need to create a $\frac{1}{4}$" × $\frac{7}{8}$" rabbet on the stiles of the face frame. I use a pattern bit with a straightedge.

9 When the case is dry, invert and slide the bottom and shelf into the case. Nail through the bottom of the pieces and into the stiles of the sides.

8 You now need to attach the face frame to the sides. Here, the rabbet helps to locate the sides with the frame.

10 Cut the rear top support to which you will attach the backboards and, using screws, install the piece. Be sure not to creep below the area that the moulding will cover.

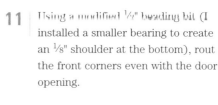

11 Using a modified ¼" beading bit (I installed a smaller bearing to create an ⅛" shoulder at the bottom), rout the front corners even with the door opening.

12 Finish the corner treatment with a chisel.

13 Mill and create the doors in much the same way you built the sides. Cut the mortises and tenons, and groove for the raised panels. After making the panels, assemble the doors and peg.

14 Fit the doors to the openings and temporarily install with the 1½" butt hinges.

15 Remove the doors and add the ¼" bead to the outer edge of the four stiles. I use a moulding-head cutter in the table saw.

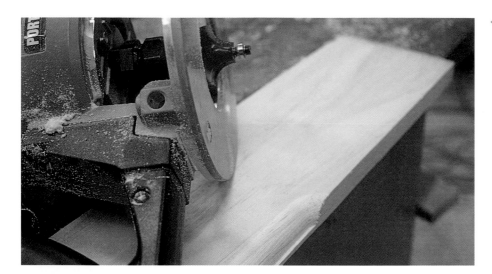

16 Using the modified beading bit, mill the top edge of the lower section base, and cut a ⅛" groove just below the profile with the table saw.

17 Fit the base to the case. Cut the decorative details in the sides and front pieces with a jigsaw or band saw, then install using reproduction nails.

18 With the biscuit joiner, cut a ¼" cut to accept the wooden clips in the sides and front face frame. (See "Wood Clips" on page 9.)

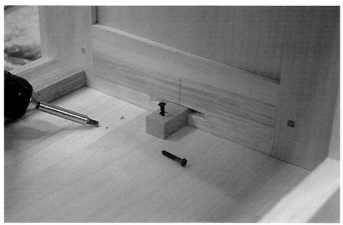

19 Mill the top to size. With the case inverted onto the top, install the clips as shown. Then simply screw the rear top support to the top with No. 8 × 1¼" wood screws.

20 Make the moulding that fits just below the top with a ½" roundover bit, then fit and attach with nails to the underside of the top.

21 Begin the same process again, this time making the upper section sides. Locate the top, bottom and sides, then cut the dadoes where needed.

22 Cut the rabbet for the backboards and add a cutout for the rear drawer support.

23 Make the upper face frame according to the plan. Use the same process you used on the lower frame. Create the 1/4" × 7/8" rabbet that allows the front corner edge treatment, as you did on the lower case. When ready, glue the frame to the sides. Allow the assembly to dry, and nail the drawer support into place. The clamp keeps the sides from moving away when nailing.

24 As before, mill the top, bottom and shelves, and install by nailing through the bottom of each piece and into the side stiles. Using a round-nose bit, add a plate groove to the top side of the bottom and the shelves. I set my center of the groove to 1½" from the back edge. Then create the front corner edge treatment as you did on the lower section.

25 Nail the drawer area cleats on the inside of the lower face frame rail and rear drawer support ½" below the top of the rail edge. Mill the runner/guide pieces. Cut a 3/8" rabbet along the appropriate edges. Then align with the face-frame locations and nail into the supports. This is a great time to build the drawers. (See "Drawer Basics: Hand-cut Dovetails" on page 8.)

26 Build the doors. Because these doors have true glass dividers, as well as a moulded inside edge, they are more involved. First cut your pieces and run the inside edge profile. I use a $^3/_{16}$" bead that later will match the cut of a $^3/_{16}$" cove. Cut the mortises according to the plan, and create the $^3/_8$" × $^5/_8$" rabbet for the glass. With the blade set to 45° and the rails on routed edge, make the cut to establish the tenon. While the blade is still set to 45°, also cut the stiles to meet the rail cut. *Note: In the photo at left my hands are close to the saw blade only to point out its 45° angle.*

27 Set the blade back to 90° and finish the tenons. Remember to offset the bottom and back sides to accommodate for the glass-area rabbet. Dry fit the rails and stiles.

28 Fine-tune any imperfections and glue the door frames, then peg the joints. Hang the doors as you did on the lower section; however, these doors need a half-lap joint at the center, so create the joint as you fit the doors to the opening.

29 After the doors are in place, mark the exact location of the shelves to ensure that the dividers align with the shelf fronts.

30 Cut the glass-divider backing, and create the glass dividers by milling the profile on a wide piece of stock and cutting the thin pieces from the edge.

31 Fit the horizontal backing pieces into the door frame at the location of each shelf.

32 Make a groove in a scrap block that just captures the glass divider and, with the piece cut to length, profile each end with the $\frac{3}{16}$" cove cutter.

33 This is how the finished pieces should look.

34 Make the center vertical divider, and glue at each end and where it crosses the horizontal backers.

35 Using the same methods, fill in the remainder of the glass grid for both doors.

36 Cut the pieces for the top moulding, and biscuit the three-sided frame together. After it is dry, then sand and profile the edge with a large Roman ogee bit. Install by screwing the piece to the upper section case top with No. $8 \times 1\frac{1}{4}$" wood screws.

37 With the case inverted, profile the Stage No. 1 moulding with a small Roman ogee bit, and nail to the case sides and front.

38 Make the dentil moulding (see "Making Dentil Moulding" on page 79) and install over the Stage No. 1 moulding.

39 Then mill the Stage No. 4 moulding to size, and create the ¼" bead detail. This moulding is applied to the top frame.

40 Make the cove that completes this bold case moulding, and mill the half-lap backboards for both the upper and lower sections of the cupboard.

41 Stack the two cases, then make and cut to fit the waist cove moulding with a ½" cove bit. Attach to the base top. I space the moulding with a sanding disc of gap to allow the upper section to easily slide into place.

Tip When moulding pieces on the edge, as in the glass dividers, it helps to group together a number of pieces of stock to allow the router base ample support.

42 | The finish I selected for this piece is an aged paint. Stain the piece with an aniline dye, sand to knock down the fuzzies and apply a coat of shellac. After I have placed a few nicks and dings in the heavily worn areas, the desired color of paint with some sawdust or vacuum dust mixed in is applied, scraped and rubbed away in areas to simulate years of wear. Finally a dark wax is applied. The interior is painted, lightly rubbed and waxed.

making dentil moulding

1

With a lengthy piece of scrap against the miter gauge and the dado blade set to the desired width and height (I use ³⁄₈" x ⁵⁄₈"), make a pass over the blade. Slide the scrap to the side to achieve the width of each tooth, which is ⁵⁄₈"; it may take a couple of attempts. When satisfied, attach the scrap to the gauge, make a second pass over the blade, then attach a small block into the first cut as shown.

2

Take the dentil stock, place the end against the attached block and make your first cut.

3

Remove the stock and slide the cut groove over the attached block to create the first tooth.

4

Simply continue the process until you have reached the necessary size and number of pieces. Then cut to final dimensions and install.

chippendale ENTERTAINMENT CENTER

THIS ENTERTAINMENT CENTER IS A FINE EXAMPLE OF THE custom furniture concept. While I was building another piece similar to this one, I was approached by a woman who commissioned me to build this particular piece. She had an idea of the design she wanted, but had not been able to find an antique that exactly matched her imagination.

After evaluating a number of different cupboards, we began to incorporate aspects of each piece and apply them to one final piece, designed specifically for her.

The inclusion of the ogee feet, and especially the fluted corner columns, help to propel this entertainment center straight to the top of its class.

FROM THE COLLECTION OF EILEEN ROBERTS, MANASSAS, VIRGINIA

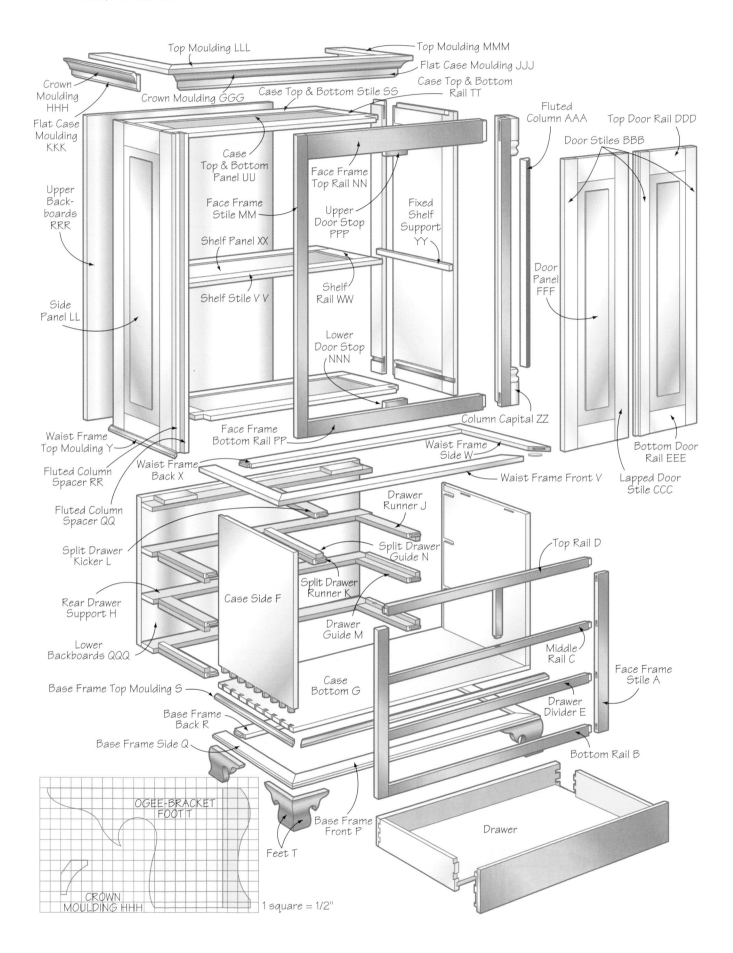

Top Moulding LLL

Top Moulding MMM

Flat Case Moulding JJJ

Crown Moulding HHH

Crown Moulding GGG

Case Top & Bottom Stile SS

Case Top & Bottom Rail TT

Fluted Column AAA

Top Door Rail DDD

Flat Case Moulding KKK

Case Top & Bottom Panel UU

Door Stiles BBB

Face Frame Top Rail NN

Upper Backboards RRR

Face Frame Stile MM

Upper Door Stop PPP

Fixed Shelf Support YY

Door Panel FFF

Shelf Panel XX

Side Panel LL

Shelf Stile V V

Shelf Rail WW

Lower Door Stop NNN

Waist Frame Top Moulding Y

Face Frame Bottom Rail PP

Column Capital ZZ

Bottom Door Rail EEE

Fluted Column Spacer RR

Waist Frame Back X

Waist Frame Side W

Waist Frame Front V

Lapped Door Stile CCC

Fluted Column Spacer QQ

Drawer Runner J

Top Rail D

Split Drawer Kicker L

Split Drawer Guide N

Rear Drawer Support H

Split Drawer Runner K

Case Side F

Drawer Guide M

Middle Rail C

Lower Backboards QQQ

Face Frame Stile A

Base Frame Top Moulding S

Case Bottom G

Drawer Divider E

Base Frame Back R

Base Frame Side Q

Bottom Rail B

OGEE-BRACKET FOOT T

Base Frame Front P

Feet T

Drawer

CROWN MOULDING HHH

1 square = 1/2"

cutting list | inches

CHIPPENDALE ENTERTAINMENT CENTER

LOWER SECTION

REFERENCE	QUANTITY	PART	STOCK	THICKNESS	WIDTH	LENGTH	COMMENTS
A	2	Front Face-Frame Stiles	P	$3/4$	2	$23^{1}/8$	
B	1	Face-Frame Bottom Rail	P	$3/4$	$1^{1}/2$	$38^{1}/2$	1" TBE
C	1	Face-Frame Middle Rail	P	$3/4$	1	$38^{1}/2$	1" TBE
D	1	Face-Frame Top Rail	P	$3/4$	$1^{1}/4$	$38^{1}/2$	1" TBE
E	1	Face-Frame Dwr. Divider	P	$3/4$	$1^{1}/4$	$8^{3}/8$	1" TBE
F	2	Case Sides	P	$3/4$	25	$23^{7}/8$	
G	1	Case Bottom	S	$5/8$	25	$40^{1}/2$	
H	3	Rear Drawer Supports	S	$3/4$	$2^{1}/4$	$39^{9}/16$	
J	6	Drawer Runners	S	$3/4$	$2^{1}/4$	$23^{1}/4$	$3/8$" TOE, 1" TOE
K	1	Split Drawer Runner	S	$3/4$	$3^{1}/4$	$23^{1}/4$	$3/8$" TOE, 1" TOE
L	1	Split Drawer Kicker	S	$3/4$	$3^{1}/4$	$23^{1}/4$	$3/8$" TOE, 1" TOE
M	6	Drawer Guides	S	$5/8$	$1^{1}/8$	19	
N	1	Split Drawer Guide	S	$5/8$	$1^{1}/4$	19	
P	1	Base Frame Front	P	$3/4$	3	$42^{3}/4$	45° BE
Q	2	Base Frame Sides	P	$3/4$	3	$26^{7}/8$	45° OE
R	1	Base Frame Back	S	$3/4$	3	$38^{3}/4$	1" TBE
S	1	Base Frame Top Moulding	P	$5/8$	$3/4$	56	cut to fit
T	2	Blanks for Feet	P	$1^{3}/8$	$5^{3}/4$	28	each blank makes three feet
U	2	Rear Foot Braces	S	$3/4$	$5^{3}/4$	7	
V	1	Waist Frame Front	P	$3/4$	3	43	45° BE
W	2	Waist Frame Sides	P	$3/4$	3	27	45° OE
X	1	Waist Frame Back	S	$3/4$	3	39	1" TBE
Y	1	Waist Frame Top Moulding	P	$5/8$	$3/4$	56	cut to fit
Z	2	Drawer Fronts	P	$13/16$	$6^{9}/16$	$18^{1}/4$	$5/16$" rabbet, three sides
AA	2	Drawer Fronts	P	$13/16$	$6^{9}/16$	$37^{1}/8$	$5/16$" rabbet, three sides
BB	8	Drawer Sides	S	$9/16$	$6^{1}/4$	20	
CC	2	Top Drawer Backs	S	$9/16$	$5^{1}/2$	$17^{1}/2$	
DD	2	Drawer Backs	S	$9/16$	$5^{1}/2$	$36^{7}/16$	
EE	2	Top Drawer Bottoms	S	$5/8$	$20^{1}/2$	$16^{7}/8$	
FF	2	Drawer Bottoms	S	$5/8$	$20^{1}/2$	$35^{7}/8$	

TBE = Tenon Both Ends

TOE = Tenon One End

TAS = Tenon All Sides

BE = Both Ends

OE = One End

UPPER SECTION

REFERENCE	QUANTITY	PART	STOCK	THICKNESS	WIDTH	LENGTH	COMMENTS
GG	2	Side Front Stiles	P	$3/4$	$2^{1}/4$	49	
HH	2	Side Rear Stiles	P	$3/4$	$3^{1}/4$	49	
JJ	2	Side Top Rails	P	$3/4$	$5^{3}/4$	20	$1^{3}/8$" TBE
KK	2	Side Bottom Rails	P	$3/4$	$4^{1}/4$	20	$1^{3}/8$" TBE
LL	2	Side Panels	P	$5/8$	$17^{7}/8$	$39^{5}/8$	
MM	2	Face-Frame Stiles	P	$3/4$	$2^{3}/4$	49	
NN	1	Face-Frame Top Rail	P	$3/4$	$5^{3}/4$	$32^{3}/4$	$1^{3}/8$" TBE
PP	1	Face-Frame Bottom Rail	P	$3/4$	$1^{1}/2$	$32^{3}/4$	$1^{3}/8$" TBE
QQ	2	Fluted Column Spacers	S	$3/4$	$1^{1}/2$	49	
RR	2	Fluted Column Spacers	S	$3/4$	$3/4$	49	
SS	4	Case Top and Bottom Stiles	S	$3/4$	$3^{1}/2$	$37^{7}/16$	
TT	4	Case Top and Bottom Rails	S	$3/4$	3	$18^{15}/16$	$1^{1}/4$" TBE
UU	2	Case Top and Bottom Panels	S	$3/4$	$17^{1}/8$	$32^{1}/8$	$3/8$" TAS
VV	6	Shelf Stiles	S	$3/4$	3	$36^{3}/4$	
WW	6	Shelf Rails	S	$3/4$	3	18	$1^{1}/4$" TBE
XX	3	Shelf Panels	S	$3/4$	$16^{1}/8$	$31^{3}/8$	$3/8$" TAS
YY	2	Fixed Shelf Supports	S	$3/4$	2	$21^{5}/8$	
ZZ	4	Column Capitals	P	$1^{1}/2$	$1^{1}/2$	9	4 pieces glue to one
AAA	4	Fluted Columns	P	$1^{1}/4$	$1^{1}/4$	36	4 pieces glue to one; need only two pieces
BBB	3	Door Stiles	P	$3/4$	$2^{3}/4$	$41^{3}/4$	
CCC	1	Lapped Door Stile	P	$3/4$	$3^{1}/8$	$41^{3}/4$	
DDD	2	Top Door Rails	P	$3/4$	$2^{3}/4$	$12^{1}/4$	$1^{3}/8$" TBE
EEE	2	Bottom Door Rails	P	$3/4$	$3^{1}/2$	$12^{1}/4$	$1^{3}/8$" TBE
FFF	2	Door Panels	P	$5/8$	$10^{1}/8$	$36^{1}/8$	
GGG	1	Crown Moulding	P	$3/4$	$2^{1}/2$	45	cut to fit
HHH	2	Crown Moulding	P	$3/4$	$2^{1}/2$	29	cut to fit
JJJ	1	Flat Case Moulding	P	$7/16$	$2^{1}/8$	40	cut to fit
KKK	2	Flat Case Moulding	P	$7/16$	$2^{1}/8$	26	cut to fit
LLL	1	Top Moulding	P	$3/4$	$3^{1}/4$	45	cut to fit
MMM	2	Top Moulding	P	$3/4$	$3^{1}/4$	29	cut to fit
NNN	1	Lower Door Stop	P	$3/4$	$3/4$	4	
PPP	1	Upper Door Stop	P	$1/2$	4	4	
QQQ	1	Lower Backboards	S	$5/8$	$23^{1}/4$	$39^{7}/8$	assembled pieces
RRR	1	Upper Backboards	S	$5/8$	48	$37^{3}/4$	assembled pieces

hardware and supplies

HORTON BRASSES HARDWARE:

Rosette pulls	6, size H-10FB, antique finish
Stirrup pulls	2, size H-40, antique finish
H-hinges	2 prs., size HH-2, 3", antique finish
Shelf supports (standard)	8, $1/4$"
Slot-head wood screws	

cutting list | millimeters

CHIPPENDALE ENTERTAINMENT CENTER

LOWER SECTION

REFERENCE	QUANTITY	PART	STOCK	THICKNESS	WIDTH	LENGTH	COMMENTS
A	2	Front Face Frame Stiles	P	19	51	606	
B	1	Face-Frame Bottom Rail	P	19	38	978	25mm TBE
C	1	Face-Frame Middle Rail	P	19	25	978	25mm TBE
D	1	Face-Frame Top Rail	P	19	32	978	25mm TBE
E	1	Face-Frame Dwr. Divider	P	19	32	213	25mm TBE
F	2	Case Sides	P	19	635	606	
G	1	Case Bottom	S	16	635	1051	
H	3	Rear Drawer Supports	S	19	57	1011	
J	6	Drawer Runners	S	19	57	590	10mm TOE, 25mm TOE
K	1	Split Dr. Runner	S	19	82	590	10mm TOE, 25mm TOE
L	1	Split Dr. Kicker	S	19	82	590	10mm TOE, 25mm TOE
M	6	Drawer Guides	S	16	29	433	
N	1	Split Drawer Guide	S	16	32	433	
P	1	Base Frame Front	P	19	76	1086	45° BE
Q	2	Base Frame Sides	P	19	76	682	45° OE
R	1	Base Frame Back	S	19	76	984	25mm TBE
S	1	Base Frame Top Moulding	P	16	19	1422	cut to fit
T	2	Blanks for Feet	P	35	146	711	each blank makes three feet
U	2	Rear Foot Braces	S	19	146	178	
V	1	Waist Frame Front	P	19	76	1092	45° BE
W	2	Waist Frame Sides	P	19	76	686	45° OE
X	1	Waist Frame Back	S	19	76	991	25mm TBE
Y	1	Waist Frame Top Moulding	P	16	19	1422	cut to fit
Z	2	Drawer Fronts	P	21	166	463	8mm rabbet, three sides
AA	2	Drawer Fronts	P	21	166	943	8mm rabbet, three sides
BB	8	Drawer Sides	S	14	158	508	
CC	2	Top Drawer Backs	S	14	140	445	
DD	2	Drawer Backs	S	14	140	925	
EE	2	Top Drawer Bottoms	S	16	521	428	
FF	2	Drawer Bottoms	S	16	521	911	

UPPER SECTION

REFERENCE	QUANTITY	PART	STOCK	THICKNESS	WIDTH	LENGTH	COMMENTS
GG	2	Side Front Stiles	P	19	70	1245	
HH	2	Side Rear Stiles	P	19	82	1245	
JJ	2	Side Top Rails	P	19	146	508	35mm TBE
KK	2	Side Bottom Rails	P	19	108	508	35mm TBE
LL	2	Side Panels	P	16	454	1007	
MM	2	Face-Frame Stiles	P	19	70	1245	
NN	1	Face-Frame Top Rail	P	19	146	832	35mm TBE
PP	1	Face-Frame Bottom Rail	P	19	38	832	35mm TBE
QQ	2	Fluted Column Spacers	S	19	38	1245	
RR	2	Fluted Column Spacers	S	19	19	1245	
SS	4	Case Top and Bottom Stiles	S	19	89	951	
TT	4	Case Top and Bottom Rails	S	19	76	481	32mm TBE
UU	2	Case Top and Bottom Panels	S	19	435	816	10mm TAS
VV	6	Shelf Stiles	S	19	76	933	
WW	6	Shelf Rails	S	19	76	457	32mm TBE
XX	3	Shelf Panels	S	19	409	797	10mm TAS
YY	2	Fixed Shelf Supports	S	19	51	549	
ZZ	4	Column Capitals	P	38	38	229	4 pieces glue to one
AAA	4	Fluted Columns	P	32	32	914	4 pieces glue to one; need only two pieces
BBB	3	Door Stiles	P	19	70	1060	
CCC	1	Lapped Door Stile	P	19	79	1060	
DDD	2	Top Door Rails	P	19	70	311	35mm TBE
EEE	2	Bottom Door Rails	P	19	89	311	35mm TBE
FFF	2	Door Panels	P	16	257	917	
GGG	1	Crown Moulding	P	19	64	1143	cut to fit
HHH	2	Crown Moulding	P	19	64	737	cut to fit
JJJ	1	Flat Case Moulding	P	11	54	1016	cut to fit
KKK	2	Flat Case Moulding	P	11	54	660	cut to fit
LLL	1	Top Moulding	P	19	82	1168	cut to fit
MMM	2	Top Moulding	P	19	82	737	cut to fit
NNN	1	Lower Door Stop	P	19	19	102	
PPP	1	Upper Door Stop	P	13	102	102	
QQQ	1	Lower Backboards	S	16	590	1013	assembled pieces
RRR	1	Upper Backboards	S	16	1219	959	assembled pieces

TBE = Tenon Both Ends

TOE = Tenon One End

TAS = Tenon All Sides

BE = Both Ends

OE = One End

hardware and supplies

HORTON BRASSES HARDWARE:

Rosette pulls	6, size H-10FB, antique finish
Stirrup pulls	2, size H-40, antique finish
H-hinges	2 prs., size HH-2, 76mm, antique finish
Shelf supports (standard)	8, 6mm
Slot-head wood screws	

1 Cut the top, middle and lower rails and the face frame sides for the lower section according to the plan, then create the mortise-and-tenon joints to connect all of the pieces.

2 Test fit the face-frame pieces and mark all areas where mortises need to be cut to accept the drawer runners and kickers.

3 With those mortises created, it is time to assemble the lower section face frame. Make sure to square the unit by checking for equal measurements on the diagonal. With the glue set, peg the joints in the face frame.

4 Take the sides of the lower section and cut on each bottom edge the pins that will match with the dovetails on the case bottom. Locate the rear drawer dividers and top drawer kicker rails on each side. Be sure to create a pair of matching sides and rout a short $3/4$" by $1/4$"-deep groove to accept the rails, then cut the $3/4$" by $1/4$"-deep rabbet for the backboards.

5 Mill the case bottom and cut the corresponding dovetails. Then assemble and glue the sides to the bottom.

6 When the side/bottom unit is dry, it is time to attach the face-frame assembly on the front edge. Pay attention to lining up the routed rear divider slots with the face frame to ensure level running drawers.

7 Mill the drawer runner pieces to size, including the tenon work, and create a pocket screw hole to attach the runner to the side of the case. Here, I built a simple jig that lays the piece at a 15° angle. Using a ¾" Forstner bit, start the hole, stopping at the appropriate level to use a No. 8 × 1¼" slot-head wood screw. Finish predrilling the hole with a smaller bit.

8 Glue the front tenon into place, and slide the rear drawer divider into the slot and over the runner's rear tenon. Then nail through the rear divider and into the case side at a slight angle.

9 Install the screw through the pocket hole and into the case side for additional support. With all the pieces in place, size, cut and install the drawer guides so they are flush with the face-frame sides. Don't forget the center guide for the split top drawers. Then sand the unit to 180 grit.

10 Mill and assemble the foot base frame by creating mortise-and-tenon joints at the back corners and biscuited 45° cuts at the front corners.

11 Make the ogee-bracket feet. (See "Ogee-Bracket Feet" on page 7.)

12 Sand the foot base frame, then fit the ogee-bracket feet to the frame with glue and corner blocks. Rout the profile on the edge of the frame.

13 After the foot base has been completed, invert the lower case unit and attach the foot assembly to the case bottom with No. 8 × 1¼" screws in the front frame. Use nails to complete the assembly. Nails allow slight movement over time, which helps keep the piece from splitting. Notice the corner blocks on the feet.

14 Next, mill and install the base moulding that covers the exposed case dovetails.

15 Make the lower section top frame just as you did the foot base frame, and cut the profile with a combination of a thumbnail bit and a $^3/_{16}$" roundover bit.

16 Nail sized filler pieces to the bottom of the top frame at the back rail, then finish sand the top frame and attach it to the lower section with wood clips (see "Wood Clips" on page 9) and screws into the filler pieces.

17 Now is the time to build the drawers for the lower section of the entertainment center. (See "Drawer Basics: Hand-cut Dovetails" on page 8.)

18 Turning to the upper section, mill the frame pieces of the sides to width; but before you cut to length, create the roundover detail on the interior edge of the pieces. Next, lay out and cut the $^1/_4$"-wide mortises in all stiles.

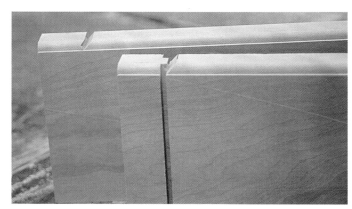

19 Set the blade to 45°. Cut just to the shoulder of the roundover cut on all rails (a single pass creates the tenon area) and stiles (nibble away for the mortises). Reset the blade to 90° and complete the tenons.

20 Adjust the fence to remove the roundover edge, and cut just up to the angle created in the piece.

21 Set the saw blade depth to ⅜" and run a ¼"-wide groove in all pieces to capture the raised panels. Check the fit and check the measurements for the panels.

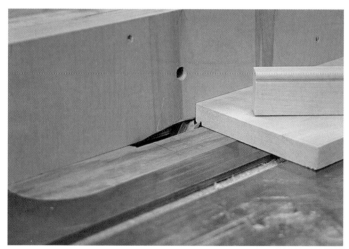

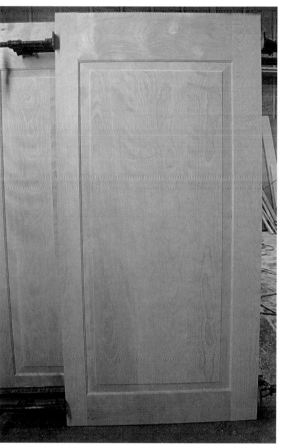

22 Mill and cut the raised panels, and when the edges have been final sanded to 180 grit, glue and assemble the side units.

23 Make the upper section front face frame just as you did the side unit frames, but without the groove for the panels. Also, use a bead detail on the interior edge instead of a roundover. This allows the doors to be framed within a beaded border.

24 When the sides are dry, locate where the top and bottom panels fit, and cut a ¾" × ¼" dado for each. Then cut the ¹⁄₁₆" × ¾" rabbet for the backboards.

25 Make the L-shape corner that will create the area for the fluted columns, and attach it to the front inside edge of the side units.

26 When set, glue the front face frame to the other leg of the L-corner, creating the quartered column area.

27 Mill, cut to size and assemble the top and bottom panels as well as the two shelves. All are made in the same fashion, with the front and back pieces being the stiles and the ends being the rails.

28 Notch the top and bottom around the L-corner to fit tightly against the face frame.

29 Once sanded, slide the top panel into the side unit dadoes. Nail through the panels into the case sides at a slight angle.

30 Locate and install a shelf cleat on each side of the upper case to hold the semi-fixed shelf in place. Use screws to attach the semi-fixed shelf to the cleats.

31 Using a piece of pegboard, drill the holes for the adjustable shelf clips that are used with the adjustable shelf. Be sure to orient the template properly. I start with the template at the top and skip down approximately 8" to the first hole, then drill every other hole. First mark the hole with a Vix bit to set the hole depth, then follow with a ¼" bit to finish. I figure a 12" adjustment area.

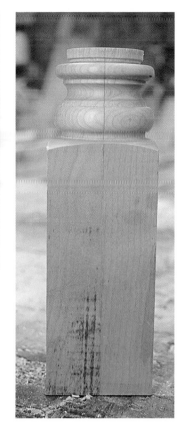

32 To make the turn-fluted quartered columns, start by gluing together four pieces of wood equal in size, in this case 1½" square by 9" in length. The trick is to place brown paper-bag paper between the pieces. After the assembled piece is dry, turn to profile.

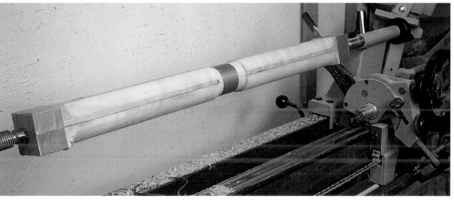

34 Assemble and turn round the pieces for the fluted portion of the columns. Place duct tape around each square end for support, then turn a place in the center to size and add tape there as well. Continue turning until the column is rounded to size, removing the tape as necessary.

33 After turning the column capitals, simply separate the pieces with a chisel and a firm tap from a mallet. For the capitals, you need to use all four resulting pieces: two at the top and two at the bottom.

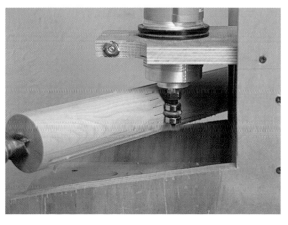

35 To flute two portions of the column, use a fluting bit in a trim router mounted in a wooden cradle layout. There will be use for only two pieces. When you're done, separate the finished pieces.

36 Install the upper capitals with glue and clamps as shown in the plan. Then cut the fluted portion of the column to size, and glue and nail the piece into place.

37 Finish the columns by cutting the base capital to size and gluing it into place.

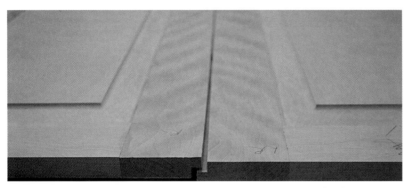

38 Make the doors just as you did the side units (see steps 18–22 on pages 88–89). Once fit to the face frame, the half-lap detail is added to the center stile on each door.

39 Create the top moulding of the cupboard using a ½" roundover bit. The moulding is attached to the case by first cutting the 45° angles on each end of the front piece and on one end of the side pieces, then biscuit cuts are made in each angle cut. Next attach the front piece with glue and screws (No. 8 × 1¼" wood screws), then fit the side pieces, glue at the biscuit areas, and screw the ends to the case.

40 Invert the case on the top and apply the first stage moulding to the case with nails. Next, make and cut the crown moulding and nail to both the case and the top moulding.

Tip Locate the holes for your particular hardware and counterbore a ⅝" hole in the backside of the drawer front with a Forstner bit. This allows the hardware to be flush on the interior of the drawer; so no snagging of your clothes!

41 Place the upper section on top of the lower section. Align the upper section into place, making it flush in the back and equally spaced on each side. Mill and cut to fit the waist moulding that is attached to the lower section with nails and that allows the upper section to slide into the three-sided space. Remember to allow a sanding disc's width between the upper case and the moulding on each side, so you can easily maneuver the large upper case. Also install the doorstop pieces shown in the center of the opening. They are at the top and bottom of the door area.

42 Now is the time to make the backboards for the cupboard. Remember that the upper section back pieces are shorter than the lower section. All pieces are half-lapped. After all of the pieces are sanded, then it's time to apply the finish (see "Lacquer Finishing" below).

lacquer finishing

To finish a piece in lacquer, first final sand the piece to 180 grit, then wet the entire piece in order to raise the grain. When dry, lightly sand a second time with the 180 grit. Next, select a water-based aniline dye stain that is mixed according to directions and thoroughly soak the piece of furniture. Allow to sit until almost dry, then remove any excess stain. Once the stain has dried, lightly sand with a 400-grit paper to knock down the "fuzzies."

Now spray a heavy coat of lacquer sanding sealer. When the sealer is dry, sand the entire piece with a 320-grit paper or a 400-grit sponge. Remove all the dust with a tack cloth.

Thin the lacquer topcoat to the desired consistency and spray several coats (usually four or five), being sure to allow drying time between each coat. If necessary, sand problem areas prior to the final coat. A single-edge razor blade helps eliminate runs or sags.

I like to use a "dull-rubbed-effect" lacquer for my pieces. I believe it best simulates an antique-style finish. I also spray with a HVLP unit.

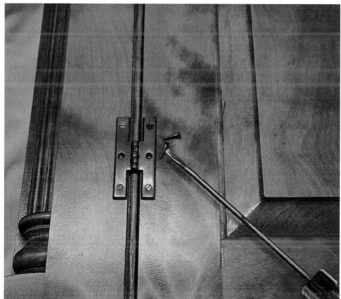

43 After you have applied the finish to the entertainment center, you need to install the appropriate hardware. Here you see the "H" hinges. Lay the hinge so that one leg of the hinge is on the door stile, with the other on the face frame. Predrill for the screws and install. Also install the rosette pulls on the drawers, the stirrup pulls on the doors and the ball catch on the doorstop at the top of the door opening.

chester county TALL CHEST

CHESTER COUNTY, PENNSYLVANIA, IS VERY WELL-KNOWN for its furniture creations. Of the many superb examples, the panel-side tall chest I've re-created here certainly stands in a class by itself.

This striking nine-drawer chest exhibits some of the most often seen features of quality Chester County craftsmanship. The three drawers at the top gracefully arch, the two drawers below feature escutcheon pulls and the paneled sides are classic in their design.

After my first encounter, I knew this tall chest must have a place in my collection.

FROM THE COLLECTION OF EDWARD BROWN, KENT, CONNECTICUT

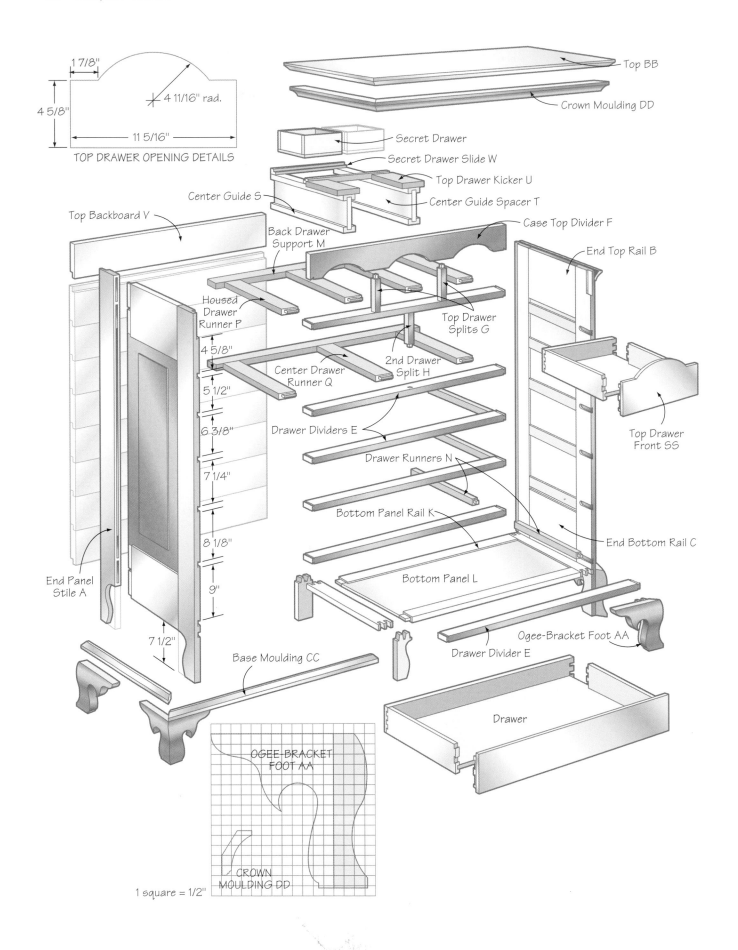

TOP DRAWER OPENING DETAILS

1 7/8"

4 5/8"

4 11/16" rad.

11 5/16"

Top BB

Crown Moulding DD

Secret Drawer

Secret Drawer Slide W

Top Drawer Kicker U

Center Guide S

Center Guide Spacer T

Top Backboard V

Case Top Divider F

Back Drawer Support M

End Top Rail B

Housed Drawer Runner P

Top Drawer Splits G

4 5/8"

Center Drawer Runner Q

2nd Drawer Split H

5 1/2"

6 3/8"

Drawer Dividers E

Top Drawer Front SS

7 1/4"

Drawer Runners N

8 1/8"

Bottom Panel Rail K

End Bottom Rail C

9"

End Panel Stile A

Bottom Panel L

Ogee-Bracket Foot AA

Drawer Divider E

7 1/2"

Base Moulding CC

Drawer

OGEE-BRACKET FOOT AA

CROWN MOULDING DD

1 square = 1/2"

cutting list | Inches

CHESTER COUNTY TALL CHEST

SIDE PANELS

REFERENCE	QUANTITY	PART	STOCK	THICKNESS	WIDTH	LENGTH	
A	4	End Panel Stiles	P	7/8	5 1/2	80	
B	2	End Top Rails	P	7/8	9	18	1 1/2" TBE
C	2	End Bottom Rails	P	7/8	10 1/2	18	1 1/2" TBE
D	2	End Panels	P	5/8	15 1/4	33 5/8	5/16" TAS
E	6	Drawer Dividers	P	7/8	2	37 1/4	1/2" dovetail ends
F	1	Case Top Divider	P	7/8	5 1/8	37 1/4	1/2" dovetail ends
G	2	Top Drawer Splits	P	7/8	1 1/8	6 3/8	7/8" TBE
H	1	Second Drawer Split	P	7/8	1 1/8	7 1/4	7/8" TBE

BOTTOM PANEL

REFERENCE	QUANTITY	PART	STOCK	THICKNESS	WIDTH	LENGTH	
J	2	Bottom Panel End Stiles	S	3/4	3	20 7/8	
K	2	Bottom Panel Rails	S	3/4	3	32 3/4	1" TBE
L	1	Bottom Panel	S	5/8	15 1/2	31 3/8	5/16" TAS
M	2	Back Drawer Supports	S	7/8	2	36 3/4	
N	8	Nailed Dwr. Runners	S	7/8	1 1/4	19	1/2" TOE
P	4	Housed Dwr. Runners	S	7/8	1 1/4	17 7/8	1/2" TBE
Q	3	Center Dwr. Runners	S	7/8	3 1/8	17 7/8	1/2" TBE
R	10	Dwr. Runner Spacers	S	1/4	1 3/8	14 1/2	
S	4	Center Guides/Secret Drawer Supports	S	3/4	1 3/8	18 1/2	
T	2	Center Guide Spacers	S	3/8	4	18 1/2	
U	2	Top Drawer Kickers	S	5/8	2 1/2	8 1/2	
V	1	Top Backboard	S	5/8	6	37 1/8	to attach top
AA	2	Ogee-Bracket Feet	P	1 5/8	7 1/2	30	
BB	1	Top	P	3/4	23 3/4	42 5/8	
CC	2	Base Moulding	P	7/8	1 1/2	48	
DD	2	Crown Moulding	P	7/8	2 1/2	48	

SECRET DRAWER PARTS

W	2	Secret Drawer Slides	S	3/4	1 1/4	13 5/8	
X	2	Secret Drawer Bottoms	S	3/8	7	6 3/4	
Y	4	Secret Drawer Pieces	S	3/8	3 5/8	5 3/4	
Z	4	Secret Drawer Pieces	S	3/8	3 5/8	6 3/4	

DRAWER PARTS

REFERENCE	QUANTITY	PART	STOCK	THICKNESS	WIDTH	LENGTH	
EE	6	Top Drawer Sides	S	1/2	4 5/6	18	
FF	4	Second Row Dwr. Sides	S	1/2	5 7/16	18	
GG	2	Drawer Sides	S	1/2	6 1/8	18	
HH	2	Drawer Sides	S	1/2	7 1/16	18	
JJ	2	Drawer Sides	S	1/2	7 7/8	18	
KK	2	Drawer Sides	S	1/2	8 7/8	18	
LL	3	Top Drawer Backs	S	1/2	3 7/8	11 5/16	
MM	2	Second Row Dwr. Backs	S	1/2	4 9/16	17 1/2	
NN	1	Drawer Backs	S	1/2	5 3/8	36 1/4	
PP	1	Drawer Backs	S	1/2	6 5/16	36 1/4	
QQ	1	Drawer Backs	S	1/2	7 1/8	36 1/4	
RR	1	Drawer Backs	S	1/2	8 1/8	36 1/4	
SS	3	Top Drawer Fronts	P	7/8	7 1/16	12	3/8" T3S
TT	2	Second Drawer Fronts	P	7/8	5 11/16	18 3/16	3/8" T3S
UU	1	Drawer Fronts	P	7/8	6 5/8	36 7/8	3/8" T3S
VV	1	Drawer Fronts	P	7/8	7 1/2	36 7/8	3/8" T3S
WW	1	Drawer Fronts	P	7/8	8 3/8	36 7/8	3/8" T3S
XX	1	Drawer Fronts	P	7/8	9 1/4	36 7/8	3/8" T3S
YY	3	Top Drawer Bottoms	S	5/8	18	10 5/8	
ZZ	2	Second Dwr. Bottoms	S	5/8	18	17	
AAA	4	Balance Dwr. Bottoms	S	5/8	18	35 5/8	
BBB	1	Backboards	S	5/8	47	37 3/16	many pieces

TBE = Tenon Both Ends

TAS = Tenon All Sides

TOE = Tenon One End

T3S = Tenon Three Sides

P = Primary Wood

S = Secondary Wood

hardware and supplies

HORTON BRASSES HARDWARE:

Drawer pulls	11, H-19L
Escutcheon pulls	2, H-19L
Escutcheon	4, H-19LE
Nails	

cutting list | millimeters

CHESTER COUNTY TALL CHEST

SIDE PANELS

REFERENCE	QUANTITY	PART	STOCK	THICKNESS	WIDTH	LENGTH	
A	4	End Panel Stiles	P	22	89	1524	
B	2	End Top Rails	P	22	229	457	38mm TBE
C	2	End Bottom Rails	P	22	267	457	38mm TBE
D	2	End Panels	P	16	387	854	24mm TAS
E	6	Drawer Dividers	P	22	51	946	13mm dovetail ends
F	1	Case Top Divider	P	22	130	946	13mm dovetail ends
G	2	Top Drawer Splits	P	22	29	162	22mm TBE
H	1	Second Drawer Split	P	22	29	190	22mm TBE

BOTTOM PANEL

J	2	Bottom Panel End Stiles	S	19	76	530	
K	2	Bottom Panel Rails	S	19	76	832	25mm TBE
L	1	Bottom Panel	S	16	394	797	8mm TAS
M	2	Back Drawer Supports	S	22	51	933	
N	8	Nailed Drawer Runners	S	22	32	483	13mm TOE
P	4	Housed Dwr. Runners	S	22	32	476	13mm TBE
Q	3	Center Drawer Runners	S	22	79	476	13mm TBE
R	10	Dwr. Runner Spacers	S	6	35	369	
S	4	Center Guides/Secret Drawer Supports	S	19	35	470	
T	2	Center Guide Spacers	S	10	102	470	
U	2	Top Drawer Kickers	S	16	64	216	
V	1	Top Backboard	S	16	152	943	to attach top
AA	2	Ogee-Bracket Feet	P	41	191	762	
BB	1	Top	P	19	597	1083	
CC	2	Base Moulding	P	22	38	1219	
DD	2	Crown Moulding	P	22	64	1219	

SECRET DRAWER PARTS

W	2	Secret Drawer Slides	S	19	32	346	
X	2	Secret Drawer Bottoms	S	10	178	171	
Y	4	Secret Drawer Pieces	S	10	92	146	
Z	4	Secret Drawer Pieces	S	10	92	171	

DRAWER PARTS

REFERENCE	QUANTITY	PART	STOCK	THICKNESS	WIDTH	LENGTH	
EE	6	Top Drawer Sides	S	13	118	457	
FF	4	Second Row Dwr. Sides	S	13	138	457	
GG	2	Drawer Sides	S	13	155	457	
HH	2	Drawer Sides	S	13	180	457	
JJ	2	Drawer Sides	S	13	200	457	
KK	2	Drawer Sides	S	13	225	457	
LL	3	Top Drawer Backs	S	13	98	287	
MM	2	Second Row Dwr. Backs	S	13	116	445	
NN	1	Drawer Backs	S	13	137	920	
PP	1	Drawer Backs	S	13	160	920	
QQ	1	Drawer Backs	S	13	181	920	
RR	1	Drawer Backs	S	13	206	920	
SS	3	Top Drawer Fronts	P	22	180	305	10mm T3S
TT	2	Second Drawer Fronts	P	22	145	462	10mm T3S
UU	1	Drawer Fronts	P	22	168	936	10mm T3S
VV	1	Drawer Fronts	P	22	191	936	10mm T3S
WW	1	Drawer Fronts	P	22	213	936	10mm T3S
XX	1	Drawer Fronts	P	22	235	936	10mm T3S
YY	3	Top Drawer Bottoms	S	16	457	270	
ZZ	2	Second Dwr. Bottoms	S	16	457	432	
AAA	4	Balance Dwr. Bottoms	S	16	457	905	
BBB	1	Backboards	S	16	1194	945	many pieces

TBE = Tenon Both Ends

TAS = Tenon All Sides

TOE = Tenon One End

T3S = Tenon Three Sides

P = Primary Wood

S = Secondary Wood

hardware and supplies

HORTON BRASSES HARDWARE:

Drawer Pulls	11, H-19L
Escutcheon Pulls	2, H-19L
Escutcheon	4, H-19LE
Nails	

1 | Mill the side panel pieces, then select the face side (outside) and create the 3/16" beaded edge.

2 | Use the step mortises method to cut the mortises into the side panel front and back stiles.

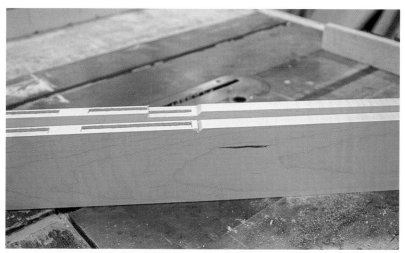

3 | With the blade set at 45°, make a cut at the line signifying the inner edge of the top and bottom rails. Slowly nibble away the material creating a working gap. (Notice the double mortise-and-tenon layout for the rails.)

4 | Change the fence setting and perform the same cuts on the rails. This time make only a single pass over the blade — no need to nibble away the material.

5 | With all the angle cuts made, straighten the blade and rip the waste away from the stiles so they're exactly even with the shoulder created with the router cut.

6 | Run the groove for the panels in both rails and stiles, then finish the tenons on the side's rails. Here you see the matching double tenons.

7 | Temporarily fit the frame pieces and double-check the panel size, then use the raised panel cutter (either on the shaper or router) to create the panel. Sand to a final sanding on the edge of the panel — the field can be sanded at a later time.

8 | With the edges of the raised panels sanded, it is time to assemble the side panels. Glue all the mortise-and-tenon joints. Be careful not to glue the panel, which is designed to float.

9 | Once the sides are dry, drill and peg the mortises.

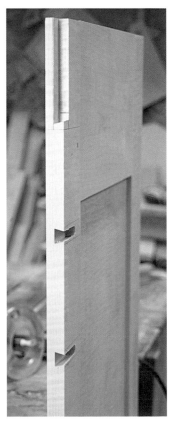

10 | Lay out the location of all the drawer dividers and, using a dovetail bit, cut a ½"-deep by 2"-long slot into the front edge of the side panels for a sliding dovetail joint. Then create a half-pin cut for the case top divider.

11 For the top two dividers, extend the layout lines to the back of the sides, and rout a ¾" × 2¾" slot for the rear dividers that contain the drawer runners for the split drawers.

12 Next, rout a ¾" rabbet at the bottom of the sides to accept the bottom partition.

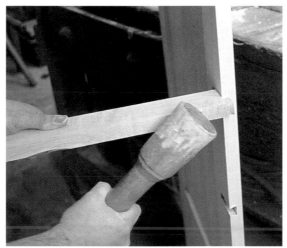

13 Create the rabbet for the chest backboards. All operations on the sides are complete.

14 Run an extra scrap piece when you mill the drawer dividers and use that to establish the correct depth and size of the dovetailed ends. Then create the matching dovetails on the ends of the dividers. Test the fit.

15 Pay close attention to the location and number of mortises in this piece. Each drawer in the top two rows requires both a face-frame piece, which is mortised into the rail above and below the divider, and a mortise for the drawer runner directly behind the divider.

16 Here you see the face-frame work for the top two rows of drawers.

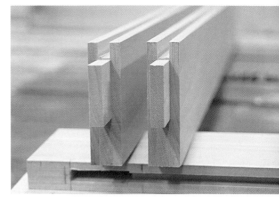

17 For the case bottom, mill the rails, stiles and panel, then create the mortise-and-tenon joints. Be sure to leave ¾" of solid material at the end of the stiles.

18 In that ¾", cut the pins for two dovetails in both ends of each stile. This is a method found on Chester County casework only and is significant in the identification of the craftsmanship.

19 Assemble the bottom panel section, and when dry, install it in the groove at the bottom of each side panel. Attach the bottom by nailing through the bottom stiles into the rabbets created in the sides.

20 Install the drawer dividers as well as the case top divider.

21 | Install the back drawer supports that have center and side runners with the ¼" spacers at the raised panel areas for the split drawers.

22 | On the center runners, mount the small I-beam design which acts as the drawer guide. Place a short runner at the front of the beam. You can add the secret drawers if you desire. The two small drawers have bottoms that slide into the profiled channel shown. They are accessible from the front only with the uppermost side drawers removed.

23 | Glue the tenons into the mortises in the front drawer dividers and nail into the side stiles at the rear.

24 | Mill the top rear case backboard and install by nailing into the sides. This piece serves two purposes: It is where the top attaches with clips and it acts as the first half-lapped backboard.

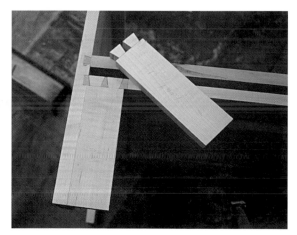

25 | Cut the matching dovetailed pieces at the feet and glue them to the lower side stiles (see step 18).

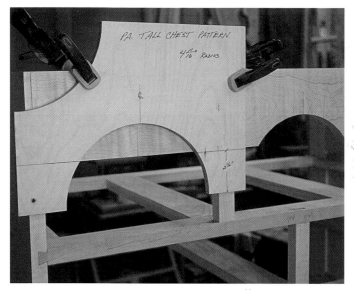

26 Mark a line with the jig — a cutout of a $4^{11}/_{16}$" radius set 2" above center — aligned with the centerline of your drawer opening. Cut the opening arch. (I like to use a pattern bit for this job.)

27 Make the ogee-bracket feet and cut away the case side stile, leaving the profile of the ogee-bracket foot. Then attach the foot assembly to the case with four No. 8 × $1^1/_4$" wood screws and glue. Attach the rear feet in the same way.

28 Use the biscuit joiner to locate and cut the slots needed to attach the top. Mill the top to size and rout the edge profile. Invert the case onto the top and attach the top with the clips as seen here. (See "Wood Clips" on page 9.)

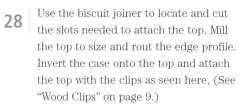

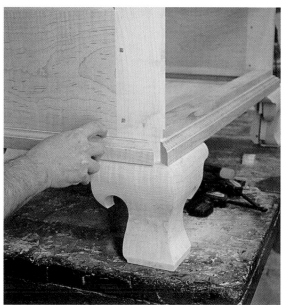

29 After sanding the case, install the crown moulding around the underside of the top. I used a shaper to detail the edge on the crown. You may create the same look by adding a third stage in the moulding (see step 40 on page 92).

30 Install the base moulding exactly above the feet by nailing the sides in place. Nail and glue the front. The case is ready for drawers.

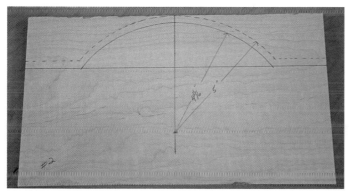

31 Build the drawers. Lay out the drawer fronts for the arched drawers and build all drawers according to the plan (see "Drawer Basics: Hand-cut Dovetails" on page 8).

32 Now for the backboards: Mill the rabbet for the half-lap joint and cut to length. I space my boards with a two-penny thickness, then mark the needed measurement and make the final cut. Final sand, and it is ready for finish.

33 After the finish is completed, install the backboards and add the hardware.

flattened shellac with glaze finish

To achieve this finish, first sand your work to 180 grit. Apply water with a towel until the grain is soaked. When the piece is dry, again sand with the 180-grit paper, saturate the piece with your selected aniline water-based dye stain, and just before the piece dries completely, wipe away the excess stain. When the stain has completely dried, lightly sand with 400-grit paper to knock down the "fuzzies," and spray three light coats of a 1 lb. cut of shellac. Sand the shellac, again with 400 grit, and add a coat of heavy-bodied glaze brushed on thinly and then removed with a rag, leaving glaze in the corners, etc., for added depth. The photo at left shows the effect that the glaze has on the furniture. When dry, seal with two additional coats of the same shellac. After allowing the shellac to thoroughly dry, sand the surface smooth with a 400-grit paper. Follow up with a topcoat of two layers of "dull-rubbed" lacquer. I like to use a dull-rubbed-effect lacquer for my pieces. I believe it best simulates an antique look in finish. I also spray with an HVLP unit.

PROJECT

9

sheraton FIELD BED

THIS FIELD BED IS BASED ON A BED originally made in northeastern Massachusetts during the early 1800s. The term *field bed* is derived from a time when these beds were carried into war camps and set up for the commanders. In order to be portable, the beds had to have the capability of breaking down completely into individual pieces.

While some professionals would be able to turn these bed posts as one piece, I have broken the posts into segments that are then joined to form the final design. Each section fits on a standard 36" lathe.

This bed has special importance to me. Although it is not the same design, the style is the same as the first bed I made at the age of 14.

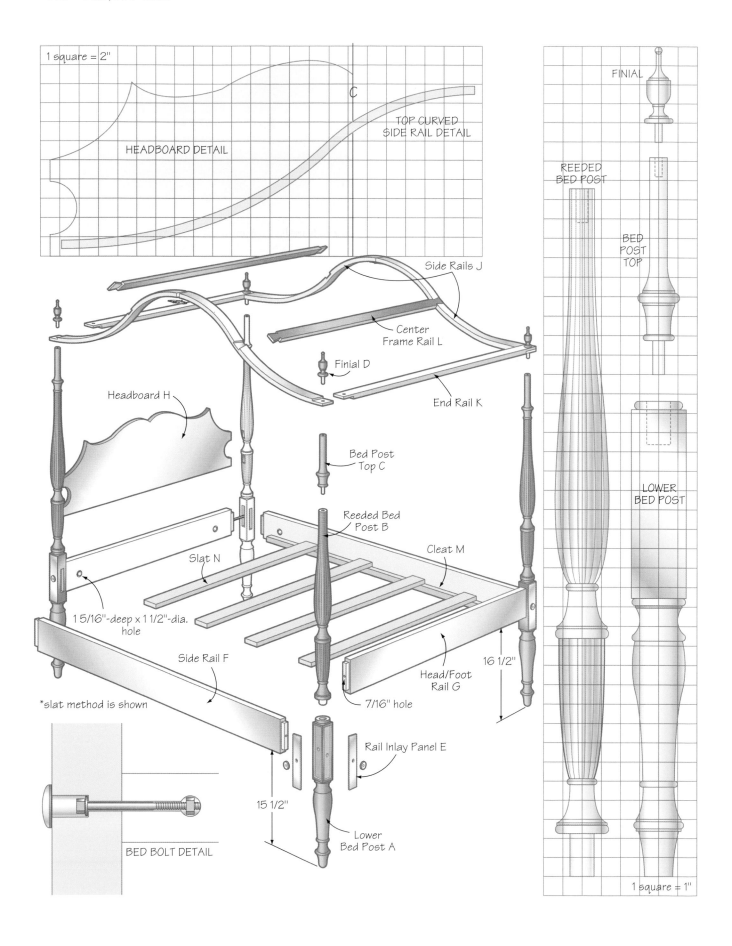

1 square = 2"

TOP CURVED
SIDE RAIL DETAIL

HEADBOARD DETAIL

C

FINIAL

REEDED
BED POST

BED
POST
TOP

Side Rails J

Center
Frame Rail L

Finial D

End Rail K

Headboard H

Bed Post
Top C

Reeded Bed
Post B

Cleat M

LOWER
BED POST

Slat N

1 5/16"-deep x 1 1/2"-dia.
hole

Side Rail F

7/16" hole

16 1/2"

*slat method is shown

Head/Foot
Rail G

Rail Inlay Panel E

15 1/2"

Lower
Bed Post A

BED BOLT DETAIL

1 square = 1"

cutting list | inches

SHERATON FIELD BED

REFERENCE	QUANTITY	PART	STOCK	THICKNESS	WIDTH	LENGTH	COMMENTS
A	4	Lower Bed Posts*	P	$2^7/_8$	$2^7/_8$	$26^1/_2$	
B	4	Reeded Bed Posts*	P	$2^1/_8$	$2^1/_8$	36	
C	4	Bed Posts Top*	P	$2^1/_4$	$2^1/_4$	13	
D	4	Finials*	P	$1^1/_2$	$1^1/_2$	8	
E	8	Rail Inlay Panels	P#2	$5/_{32}$	$2^3/_8$	$8^5/_8$	BEM
F	2	Side Rails	P	$1^5/_8$	$5^5/_8$	$81^1/_4$	$5/_8$" TBE
G	2	Head and Foot Rails	P	$1^5/_8$	$5^5/_8$	$61^1/_4$	$5/_8$" TBE
H	1	Headboard*	P	$7/_8$	18	65	

CANOPY FRAME

J	2	Side Rails	S	$1^1/_2$	5	50	each piece contains two rails
K	2	End Rails	S	$7/_8$	$1^1/_2$	$64^3/_8$	
L	2	Center Frame Rails	S	$7/_8$	$1^5/_{16}$	$64^3/_8$	

SLAT SYSTEM PIECES IF USED

M	2	Rail Cleats	S	$5/_8$	$5/_8$	74	
N	4	Slats	S	$3/_4$	$3^3/_4$	$61^3/_8$	

*Additional length included

hardware and supplies

2" Light strap hinges   1pr.

HORTON BRASSES HARDWARE:

Bed bolts	8 pcs., H-73, 6"
Bolt covers	6 pcs., BC-10
Bed wrench	BW-3
Bed irons (if used),	8 pcs., H-550 (three on either side, one on each end)

This is how your bed will look if you choose to build it without the canopy.

cutting list | millimeters

SHERATON FIELD BED

REFERENCE	QUANTITY	PART	STOCK	THICKNESS	WIDTH	LENGTH	COMMENTS
A	4	Lower Bed Posts*	P	73	73	673	
B	4	Reeded Bed Posts*	P	73	73	914	
C	4	Bed Posts Top*	P	57	57	330	
D	4	Finials*	P	38	38	203	
E	8	Rail Inlay Panels	P#2	4	61	194	BEM
F	2	Side Rails	P	41	143	2063	16mm TBE
G	2	Head and Foot Rails	P	41	143	1555	16mm TBE
H	1	Headboard*	P	22	457	1651	

CANOPY FRAME

J	2	Side Rails	S	38	127	1270	each piece contains two rails
K	2	End Rails	S	22	38	1636	
L	2	Center Frame Rails	S	22	33	1636	

SLAT SYSTEM PIECES IF USED

M	2	Rail Cleats	S	16	16	1880	
N	4	Slats	S	19	95	1559	

*Additional length included

hardware and supplies

51mm Light strap hinges 1pr.

HORTON BRASSES HARDWARE:

Bed bolts	8 pcs., H-73, 152mm
Bolt covers	6 pcs., BC-10
Bed wrench	BW-3
Bed irons (if used),	8 pcs., H-550 (three on either side, one on each end)

BEM = Bird's-Eye Maple

TBE = Tenon Both Ends

P = Primary Wood

S = Secondary Wood

1 Begin by milling all the post stock. Take the reeded post-section pieces and lay out the largest circle possible on an end. Using the jointer or table saw, remove the excess material. Do not perform this step on the lower post section because of the square area where the rails intersect.

2 Mount the reeded section into the lathe and turn the profile according to the plan.

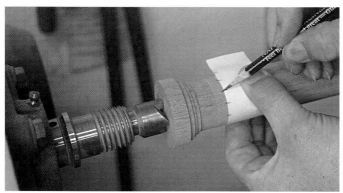

3 With the profile turned and lightly sanded, mark for the reeds. Pick a smaller-diameter area on the piece, wrap a strip of paper around the stock and mark where the paper intersects with itself. Remove the paper and divide the total measurement into 12 sections. Rewrap the paper and mark each of the divisions.

4 Build a simple jig to hold your pencil at the point of the drive center of the lathe. Mark a line along the two reeded areas on each post at each of the 12 points.

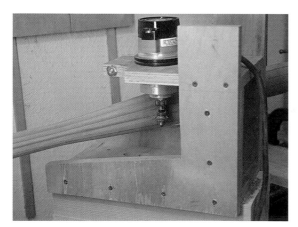

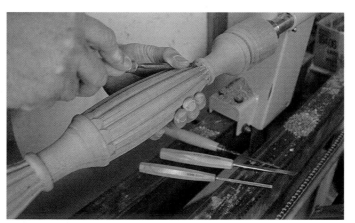

5 Create the reeds. I built an L-shape jig to hold a trim router and a reeding bit. You can also cut these reeds by hand.

6 Complete the other turned areas by hand with a few carving tools. I use a small V-groove, straight and skew chisels. At the tail-stock end, turn a $1\frac{1}{2}" \times 2\frac{1}{4}"$ tenon that will join the lower post section. At the drive end, turn any additional stock to the same $1\frac{1}{2}"$ size.

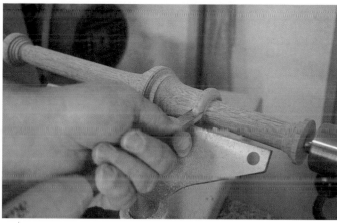

7 After the reeded post section has been completed, mount and turn the lower section according to the plan. Be careful not to knock off the corners of the square area. To prevent this from happening, I use a backsaw to make a cut.

8 The final piece of the post is the top section. While turning this section to size, leave a $\frac{5}{8}" \times 1\frac{3}{4}"$ tenon that will join into the reeded section of the post.

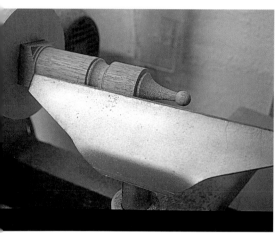

9 Turn the finial. To create the ball top, I mount a $\frac{3}{4}"$ piece of cabinet-grade plywood onto the face plate of the lathe. The plywood has a square recess cut in it that exactly fits the squared stock for the finials. Slide the stock into place and attach using a screw through the middle of the plate into the stock. The square recess acts as a drive center for the turning. With a bit of care, turn the finial to design.

10 Next, join the parts to create the posts. I turned the table of the drill press to 90° and used a plumb bob to locate the exact point of the bit. Then drill the $1\frac{1}{2}"$ hole into a scrap that is attached to the base. Without moving the drill press head, attach a piece (with the same $1\frac{1}{2}"$ hole cut into it) to the table and in line with the bottom hole. Slide the bottom tenon into the lower hole and locate the top of the post section in the upper hole. Brace in place and cut the $\frac{5}{8}"$ hole to accept the post top section tenon.

11 Attach a straightedge block to the table (I used large molly bolts). As you clamp the lower post section in place, be sure that the post is plumb and the center of the post is lined up directly with the drill bit. When ready, drill the $1\frac{1}{2}"$ hole for the reeded section tenon. Now is the time to trim any additional length and dry fit the tenons into their respective holes.

12 Lay out and cut the 1" × 5$\frac{1}{16}$" × $\frac{9}{16}$" mortises for the rails in the square area of the lower post sections. The mortises for the long rails begin at 15$\frac{1}{2}$" off the floor, and the mortises for the head-and-foot rails begin at 16$\frac{1}{2}$" off the floor.

13 Make a template for the maple inlay panels with a leg on one side to clamp to the post. Using an inlay kit, first rout an area to allow entry into the cut area, then cut the edge of the inlay recess on the opposite sides from the mortises. Remove the template and clean the recess area with a straight-bit set to the depth of the inlay bit. Follow the kit directions to create the inlay pieces and glue into place.

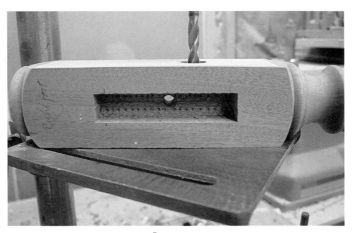

14 Return to the drill press to cut the 1" hole that will recess the head of the bed bolt. Drill about $\frac{7}{8}$" deep directly in the middle of each mortise. Notice the offset of the holes in the photo.

15 Finish the hole with a $\frac{7}{16}$" bit. Drill into the mortise area.

16 Create the 1" × 5" × $\frac{5}{8}$" tenon on each end of all four rails. I made a square box that slides onto the end of the rails and guides my router.

17 Because we offset the mortises for the long and short rails, all the holes on each rail are located in the center of the rail. First measure 3" in from the shoulder of the tenon (when using the 6" bed bolts), then drill a 1$\frac{1}{2}$" hole in the center of the rail at that spot. Drill 1$\frac{5}{16}$" deep.

18 | Examine your lower posts; determine which ones are foot and head posts, then determine left and right. Start at the left head post (as seen from the foot of the bed) and begin numbering your mortises. The head rail numbers are I and II, the right rail is III and IV, etc. Lay out the rails the same way. Clamp a lower post to the corresponding rail, then drill a $^7/_{16}$" hole into the rail using the hole you drilled in the post as a guide. The new hole will enter into the $1^1/_2$" hole drilled into the rails. This is how the bed bolt makes the connection.

Tip To turn to an accurate size (as we did for the tenons on the reeded section of the posts), cut a slot in a scrap piece of cabinet-grade plywood to the exact size needed. Then continue to turn until the slot slides onto the tenon. Each tenon will be equal in size to the drilled holes used to assemble the posts.

19 | With all the post/rail connections complete and assembled, select the locations for the reeded post sections, i.e., head or foot, and glue the two sections together. Also, glue the reeded and top sections together.

20 | Mill the headboard to size, apply the layout according to the plan and cut the profile. Sand all edges smooth.

21 | Prepare to make the headboard mortises. The lower mortise on each post begins at $31^1/_4$" above the floor. Mark for the $^7/_8$" × $2^1/_4$" × $1^1/_2$" and begin the process by drilling a series of holes with a $^5/_8$" flat-bottom bit. Work the slot to size using chisels.

22 With the lower mortise cut, gently slide the lower half of the headboard tenon into the mortise. Carefully mark for the top and bottom of the upper mortise. Remember to oversize this measurement to account for movement of the headboard. I use $\frac{3}{16}$" extra at the bottom if it is summer and at the top if it is winter.

23 To mark the exact sides of the upper mortise, slide a block that matches the size of the headboard into the slot. Using a straightedge along each side, mark the side of the top mortise. Then cut away the material as you did for the lower mortise.

24 Reassemble your head posts and rail. Using a square set on the rail at the end against the post block, measure the distance to the bottom of your mortise. Add the smallest measurement to the 60" between the posts to determine the overall length of the headboard. Then lay out the final size from a centerline in the headboard and cut to length.

25 For the canopy frame, lay out the pattern from the drawings onto the stock and carefully cut on the band saw.

26 Group the pieces together and sand both flat sides.

27 Set up and cut the arched portion of the canopy to the required size.

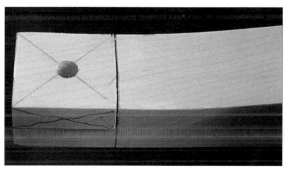

29 Mill the canopy end rails. Mark, drill and create the matching half-lap joints on the rails. This can be accomplished on a table saw or by hand.

28 Cut the half lap joints on the ends of the arched pieces, cross the corners to locate the center and drill a ³⁄₈" hole. Because of the curvature, the best way to cut these is by hand with a backsaw.

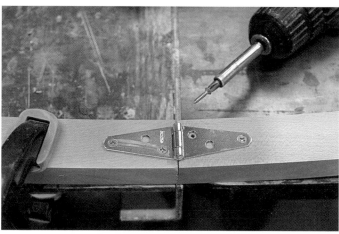

30 At the same time you create the half lap for the end rails, do the half-lap work on the center frame rails of the canopy. With the half laps complete, make a single dovetail at each end of the rails. At 31" from the post on each arched rail, clamp the dovetailed rails and transfer the dovetail to the arched piece. Then finish the joint and label each piece for later assembly.

31 The last step on the canopy is to join the arched rails with the small strap hinge. At finish time, this hinge is blackened with gun bluing, as are the screws, to simulate age.

32 This photo shows two examples of how the mattress and box springs are set into a bed. The example on the left shows the old-style bed irons. They are screwed on either long rail (three per rail) and there is a single iron set at the center of the head and foot rails. The mattress units are then set into place. The method shown on the right utilizes a cleat glued and screwed to the long rails. Then a series of four slats are spaced along that cleat, and the mattress unit is set into place. The irons present the proper reproduction views, but some of today's box springs are not strong enough to prevent sagging in the center. The slats solve that problem, but are not appropriate historically. The choice is yours.

33 Predrill for the bed-bolt covers and apply the finish. I chose to stain and lacquer finish the bed. (See "Lacquer Finishing" on page 93.)

seymour SIDEBOARD

I N THE WORLD OF ANTIQUES, THE TERMS *FEDERAL*

furniture and *Seymour* are inextricably linked. The father and

son team of John and Thomas Seymour of Boston, Massachu-

setts, have by far the most coveted name to come out of that era.

This sideboard (or mixing board, due to its marble top), typ-

ifies their work. Two design elements point directly to the Sey-

mour style: the use of the tambour doors in alternating tiger

maple and mahogany strips, and the tiger maple inlay set into

the perimeter of the tabletop and case bottom. The Hepplewhite-

style cuffed foot leads experts to believe this piece may have

been created prior to the Seymours' arrival in Boston; possibly

around 1790, when the Seymours resided in Portland, Maine.

This is a great piece to initiate (or expand) your knowledge

of inlay and shop-made veneer work.

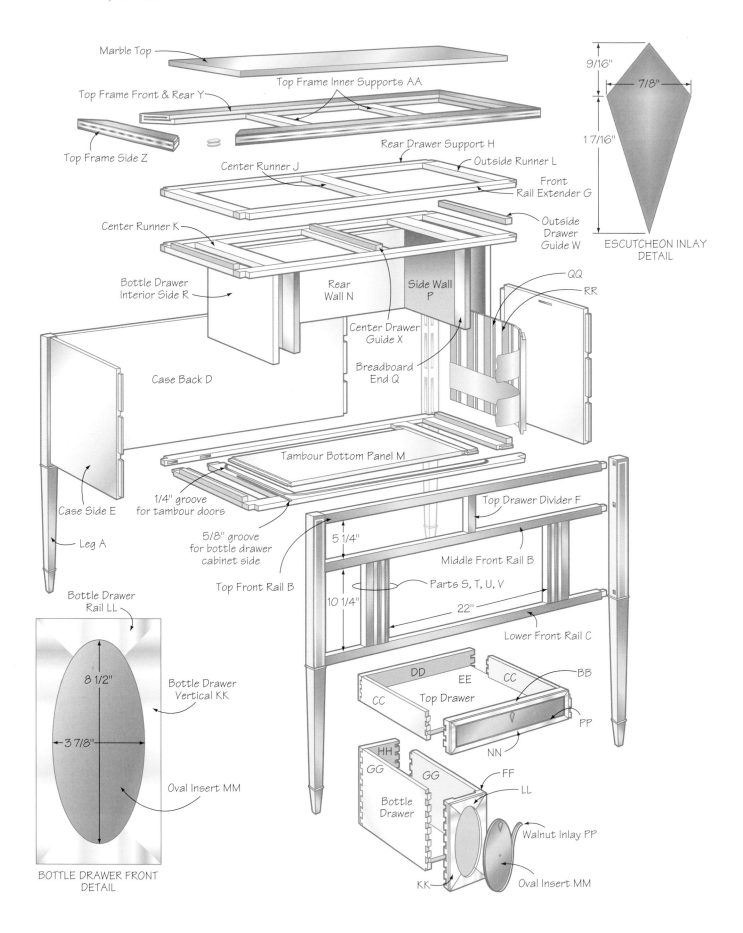

Marble Top

Top Frame Inner Supports AA

Top Frame Front & Rear Y

Top Frame Side Z

Rear Drawer Support H

Center Runner J

Outside Runner L

Front Rail Extender G

Center Runner K

Outside Drawer Guide W

Bottle Drawer Interior Side R

Rear Wall N

Side Wall P

QQ

RR

Center Drawer Guide X

Case Back D

Breadboard End Q

Case Side E

Leg A

Tambour Bottom Panel M

1/4" groove for tambour doors

Top Drawer Divider F

5/8" groove for bottle drawer cabinet side

5 1/4"

Middle Front Rail B

Top Front Rail B

Parts S, T, U, V

10 1/4"

22"

Lower Front Rail C

Bottle Drawer Rail LL

DD

EE

CC

BB

CC

Top Drawer

PP

NN

Bottle Drawer Vertical KK

8 1/2"

HH

GG

GG

FF

LL

3 7/8"

Bottle Drawer

Oval Insert MM

Walnut Inlay PP

KK

Oval Insert MM

BOTTLE DRAWER FRONT DETAIL

9/16"

7/8"

1 7/16"

ESCUTCHEON INLAY DETAIL

cutting list | inches

SEYMOUR SIDEBOARD

REFERENCE	QUANTITY	PART	STOCK	THICKNESS	WIDTH	LENGTH	
A	4	Legs	PM	$1^5/8$	$1^5/8$	$37^7/8$	
B	2	Top & Middle Front Rail	PM	$13/16$	$13/16$	$41^3/4$	$3/4$" TBE
C	1	Lower Front Rail	PM	$13/16$	$1^1/8$	$41^3/4$	$3/4$" TBE
D	1	Case Back	PM	$13/16$	$18^1/4$	$41^3/4$	$3/4$" TBE
E	2	Case Sides	PM	$13/16$	$18^1/4$	$21^3/4$	$3/4$" TBE
F	1	Top Drawer Divider	PM	$13/16$	$3/4$	$6^1/4$	$1/2$" TBE
G	3	Front Rail Extenders	PM	$13/16$	$1^3/8$	$41^1/2$	notch over legs
H	3	Rear Drawer Supports	S	$13/16$	$2^1/2$	$41^1/2$	notch over legs
J	2	Top Drawer Center Runner and Kicker	S	$13/16$	$2^1/4$	19	$3/4$" TOE, $1/2$" TOE
K	4	Bottle Drawer Center Runner and Kicker	S	$13/16$	4	19	$3/4$" TOE, $1/2$" TOE
L	4	Bottle Drawer Outside Runner and Kicker	S	$13/16$	$1^5/8$	19	$3/4$" TOE, $1/2$" TOE
M	1	Tambour Bottom Panel	S	$13/16$	17	$23^9/16$	$3/8$" × $1/4$" tongue three sides

INTERIOR FRAME FOR TAMBOUR

N	1	Rear Wall	S	$3/4$	$10^1/4$	$23^1/2$	
P	2	Side Walls	S	$3/4$	$10^1/4$	16	1" breadboard ends at front
Q	2	Breadboard Ends	S	$3/4$	$1^3/8$	$10^1/4$	
R	2	Bottle Drawer Interior Sides	S	$5/8$	$11^1/2$	$10^9/16$	

TAMBOUR AREA FACE-FRAME PIECES

S	2	Face-Frame Pieces	PM	$7/8$	$1^1/8$	$11^1/4$	$1/2$" TBE
T	4	Face-Frame Pieces	PM	$7/8$	$3/4$	$11^1/4$	$1/2$" TBE
U	4	Face-Frame Pieces	PT	$7/8$	$1/2$	$11^1/4$	$1/2$" TBE
V	4	Face-Frame Pieces	PT	$7/8$	$3/16$	$11^1/4$	$1/2$" TBE
W	4	Outside Drawer Guides	S	$1/2$	$11/16$	18	
X	1	Center Drawer Guide	S	$1/2$	$3/4$	18	

TOP FRAME PIECES

Y	2	Front and Rear	PM	$11/16$	$2^1/2$	45	
Z	2	Sides	PM	$11/16$	$2^1/2$	$24^3/4$	45° angle at ends
AA	2	Inner Supports	S	$7/16$	3	$19^3/4$	

DRAWER PIECES

REFERENCE	QUANTITY	PART	STOCK	THICKNESS	WIDTH	LENGTH
BB	2	Top Drawer Fronts	PM	$7/8$	$5^1/16$	$19^5/8$
CC	4	Top Drawer Sides	PM	$7/16$	$5^3/16$	18
DD	2	Top Drawer Backs	PM	$7/16$	$4^7/16$	$19^5/8$
EE	2	Top Drawer Bottoms	S	$1/2$	$18^1/4$	$19^1/4$
FF	2	Bottle Drawer Fronts	PM	$7/8$	$10^3/16$	$5^3/16$
GG	4	Bottle Drawer Sides	PM	$7/16$	$10^3/16$	18
HH	2	Bottle Drawer Backs	PM	$7/16$	$9^7/16$	$5^3/16$
JJ	2	Bottle Drawer Bottoms	S	$1/2$	$18^1/4$	$4^3/4$

DRAWER FACE VENEERS

KK	4	Bottle Drawer Verticals	PT	$5/8$	$2^1/2$	$10^1/4$	45° angle at ends
LL	4	Bottle Drawer Rails	PT	$5/8$	$2^1/2$	$5^1/4$	45° angle at ends
MM	2	Oval Inserts	PM	$1/2$	$4^1/2$	$9^1/2$	
NN	6	Top Drawer Banding	PT	$5/32$	$7/8$	20	
PP	12lf	Walnut Stripping					

TAMBOUR DOORS (EXTRA 5 PIECES PER COMBINATION)

QQ	20	$1/2$" Mahogany with $1/8$" Tiger Maple		$1/2$	$5/8$	$11^1/4$
RR	20	$1/2$" Tiger Maple with $1/8$" Mahogany		$1/2$	$5/8$	$11^1/4$
SS	1	Pull Pieces	PM	$5/8$	$1^3/8$	$10^1/4$
TT	1	Pull Pieces	PT	$5/8$	$1^3/8$	$10^1/4$
UU	1	Flat Inlay for Pulls	PT	$5/32$	$5/8$	$10^1/4$
VV	1	Flat Inlay for Pulls	PM	$5/32$	$5/8$	$10^1/4$

MISCELLANEOUS INLAY AND BANDING

WW	8lf	Top Upper Band	PT	$1/8$	$5/16$	
XX	8lf	Top Lower Band		$1/8$	$1/4$	store-bought
YY	8lf	Lower Case Band	PT	$5/32$	$1/4$	
ZZ	2lf	Foot Cuff	PT	$5/32$	$1/4$	
AAA	8lf	Front Leg Inlay	PT	$5/32$	$1/8$	

TBE = Tenon Both Ends
TOE = Tenon One End
PM = Primary Wood: Mahogany
PT = Primary Wood: Tiger Maple
S = Secondary Wood

hardware and supplies

HORTON BRASSES HARDWARE:

Top drawer pulls	4 pcs., $2^1/2$" bore, H-3
Bottle drawer pulls	2 pcs., $1^1/2$", H 30
Tambour door lock	LK-19
Marble	$3/4$" x $11/16$" x $21^7/16$", 1 piece
Bottle drawer locks	2, LK-4

No. 8 x $1^1/4$" slot-head wood screw

No. 10 x 1" slot-head wood screw

cutting list | millimeters

SEYMOUR SIDEBOARD

REFERENCE	QUANTITY	PART	STOCK	THICKNESS	WIDTH	LENGTH	
A	4	Legs	PM	41	41	950	
B	2	Top & Middle Front Rail	PM	21	21	1060	19mm TBE
C	1	Lower Front Rail	PM	21	29	1060	19mm TBE
D	1	Case Back	PM	21	463	1060	19mm TBE
E	2	Case Sides	PM	21	463	552	19mm TBE
F	1	Top Drawer Divider	PM	21	19	158	13mm TBE
G	3	Front Rail Extenders	PM	21	35	1054	notch over legs
H	3	Rear Drawer Supports	S	21	64	1054	notch over legs
J	2	Top Drawer Center Runner and Kicker	S	21	57	483	19mm TOE, 13mm TOE
K	4	Bottle Drawer Center Runner and Kicker	S	21	102	483	19mm TOE, 13mm TOE
L	4	Bottle Drawer Outside Runner and Kicker	S	21	41	483	19mm TOE, 13mm TOE
M	1	Tambour Bottom Panel	S	21	432	598	10mm × 6mm tongue three sides

INTERIOR FRAME FOR TAMBOUR

N	1	Rear Wall	S	19	260	597	
P	2	Side Walls	S	19	260	406	25mm breadboard ends at front
Q	2	Breadboard Ends	S	19	35	260	
R	2	Bottle Drawer Interior Sides	S	16	292	268	

TAMBOUR AREA FACE-FRAME PIECES

S	2	Face-Frame Pieces	PM	22	29	285	13mm TBE
T	4	Face-Frame Pieces	PM	22	19	285	13mm TBE
U	4	Face-Frame Pieces	PT	22	13	285	13mm TBE
V	4	Face-Frame Pieces	PT	3	5	285	13mm TBE
W	4	Outside Drawer Guides	S	13	18	457	
X	1	Center Drawer Guide	S	13	19	457	

TOP FRAME PIECES

Y	2	Front and Rear	PM	18	64	1143	
Z	2	Sides	PM	18	64	629	45° angle at ends
AA	2	Inner Supports	S	11	76	502	

DRAWER PIECES

REFERENCE	QUANTITY	PART	STOCK	THICKNESS	WIDTH	LENGTH	
BB	2	Top Drawer Fronts	PM	22	132	499	
CC	4	Top Drawer Sides	PM	11	132	457	
DD	2	Top Drawer Backs	PM	11	115	499	
EE	2	Top Drawer Bottoms	S	13	463	489	
FF	2	Bottle Drawer Fronts	PM	22	259	132	
GG	4	Bottle Drawer Sides	PM	11	259	457	
HH	2	Bottle Drawer Backs	PM	11	240	132	
JJ	2	Bottle Drawer Bottoms	S	13	463	121	

DRAWER FACE VENEERS

KK	4	Bottle Drawer Verticals	PT	16	64	260	45° angle at ends
LL	4	Bottle Drawer Rails	PT	16	64	133	45° angle at ends
MM	2	Oval Inserts	PM	13	115	242	
NN	6	Top Drawer Banding	PT	4	22	508	
PP	12lf	Walnut Stripping					

TAMBOUR DOORS (EXTRA 5 PIECES PER COMBINATION)

QQ	20	13mm Mahogany with 3mm Tiger Maple		13	16	285	
RR	20	13mm Tiger Maple with 3mm Mahogany		13	16	285	
SS	1	Pull Pieces	PM	16	35	260	
TT	1	Pull Pieces	PT	16	35	260	
UU	1	Flat Inlay for Pulls	PT	4	16	260	
VV	1	Flat Inlay for Pulls	PM	4	16	260	

MISCELLANEOUS INLAY AND BANDING

WW	8lf	Top Upper Band	PT	3	8		
XX	8lf	Top Lower Band		3	6		store-bought
YY	8lf	Lower Case Band	PT	4	6		
ZZ	2lf	Foot Cuff	PT	4	6		
AAA	8lf	Front Leg Inlay	PT	4	3		

TBE = Tenon Both Ends

TOE = Tenon One End

PM = Primary Wood: Mahogany

PT = Primary Wood: Tiger Maple

S = Secondary Wood

hardware and supplies

HORTON BRASSES HARDWARE:

Top drawer pulls	4 pcs., 64mm bore, H-3
Bottle drawer pulls	2 pcs., 38mm, H-30
Tambour door lock	LK-19
Marble	19mm x 18mm x 544mm, 1 piece
Bottle drawer locks	2, LK-4

No. 8 x 32mm slot-head wood screw

No. 10 x 25mm slot-head wood screw

1 | Begin by cutting the leg stock to size. Because these legs are tapered on four sides, I used a method I learned from the editors of *Popular Woodworking* magazine. First, mark the leg for the needed taper; remember that there is also a small second taper at the foot. Set the jointer to cut one-half the depth, and run the cut to one-half the total taper in length.

2 | Flip the leg end for end and push the cut end flat to the table to create a "wheelie," then run the piece over the jointer again. The result is a perfect taper. Repeat this process on all four sides of each leg.

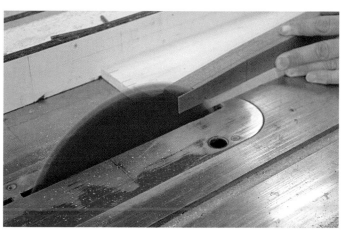

3 | Use a small tapering jig (I use a shop-made jig of plywood) to complete the tapering that forms the final foot size from the cuff to the floor.

4 | Locate and mill the necessary leg mortises for the sides and the back and front dividers.

5 | By leveling the leg onto a table saw with a couple of shims, create the 1/4" shallow recess for the cuff inlay. Cut the pieces, and inlay into the cuff.

6 | By using straightedges and a 1/8" straight bit, mill the recesses for the strip inlay on the front of the front legs. Cut the thin strips and glue them into place. A little persuasion may be necessary for a snug fit. When dry, sand the leg front smooth.

8 Mill the back, ends and front rails, and make the matching tenons. Don't forget to mortise for the drawer dividers. The top divider has to be mortised into the top and middle rails, and the bottle drawer dividers into the middle and lower rails.

7 Arrange and assemble the bottle drawer/tambour dividers as shown. When dry, create the ⅛" groove on the table saw, and inlay the tiger-maple strips to complete the divider.

9 Check the fit of the front rails, back and sides, then glue the back and front sections. Do not glue the sides at this time.

10 Make the front rail extenders and the rear drawer supports. They notch over the legs and have to be mortised for all runners and kickers.

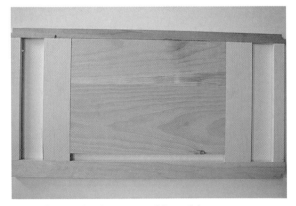

11 Create the three assemblies of drawer runners and kickers (top, middle and lower), and remember that the lower unit has a floating flat panel that acts as the tambour area bottom and is housed on three sides only. The gap created in the back is necessary for installing the tambour doors.

12 Make a pattern for the tambour door groove; an identical cut must be made on the top side of the lower unit as well as the bottom side of the middle unit. Create a half pattern and flip it for the opposite side. Use a 2"-radius corner on the pattern. Mill the ¼" × ⁵⁄₁₆" groove with a straight bit and a collar running against the pattern. Be sure the grooves meet exactly in the front and exit the runner area at the back, inside the opening created by the floating panel on the bottom assembly. Make a sample of the groove on a scrap board.

13 Rout the ⅝" groove into the top of the lower and the bottom side of the middle assembly for the bottle drawers' center runners, which are flush with the face-frame dividers.

14 Remove a ⁵⁄₁₆" portion of the underside of the middle assembly as shown for tambour installation.

15 Create the breadboard ends on the two side walls of the interior frame of the tambour area. Nail the ends to the back wall, locate the position, attach to the runners of the bottom assembly only with No. 8 × 1¼" wood screws. Use a single nail through the floating panel into the back wall for support.

16 Slide the bottle drawer interior sides into the grooves and attach with screws near the front edge. Lay the middle assembly onto the tambour area (top up) and slide the bottle drawer sides into the grooves. Attach with a single screw into the drawer sides, and use two screws to attach the tambour area walls.

17 With the back of the piece on your work surface, set the tambour cupboard section into place, and attach it to the back with glue and small glue blocks on the underside of each frame.

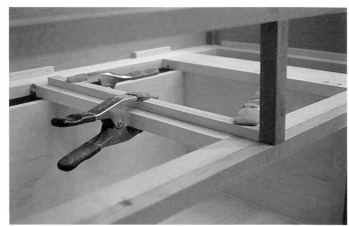

18 Glue the sides into place, clamp and square the case. Do not glue the front face frame yet. When dry, space the front face frame away from the case with a small wedge and work glue into the necessary areas. Remove the wedges, and clamp the face frame to the case. With the amount that needs to be glued, it is necessary to take this extra step.

19 Install the drawer guides for the top drawers and bottle drawers while you have easy access to those pieces. Then install the top assembly by gluing the front and rear to the case.

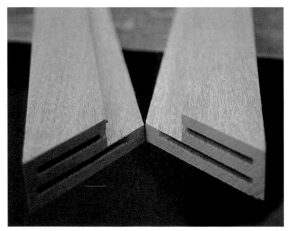

20 Mill the pieces for the top framework according to the plan. Cut the $^7/_8$" × $^5/_8$" rabbet on the inside edge, and use a biscuit joiner to create the joints for the corners as well as the inner supports. Make a double biscuit at the corners.

21 Clamp the pieces into place and allow to dry, then final sand the framework.

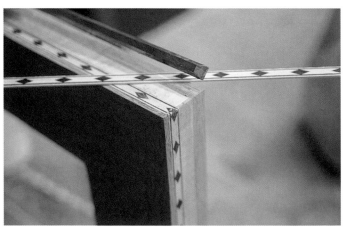

22 Create a $^5/_{16}$" groove along the front and sides of the top frame for the shop-cut inlay of tiger maple. Cut a matching inlay and glue into position.

23 When that inlay is dry, repeat the process directly below the first inlay for the designed inlay. By accomplishing this in steps, you create a seamless joint between the two inlays. When the inlay is completed, attach the top frame to the case with 1" wood screws through the rabbet area into the top front rail extender and rear drawer support.

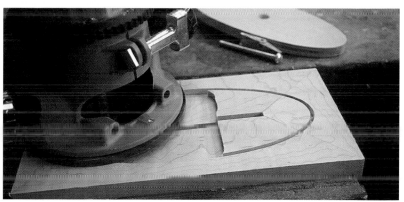

24 Create a ¼" groove at the bottom edge of the front and sides for another shop-cut inlay.

25 Cut the bottle drawer face veneer pieces, and glue them into a frame. Make the oval pattern with a scrap of plywood, install it with a large toggle bolt through the center of where the knob will mount, and place a nail towards the top edge where the material will later be removed for the diamond inlay. Using an inlay bit with the bushing off, simply run around the outside edge of the pattern. Remove the pattern and, using a router, carefully remove the waste material.

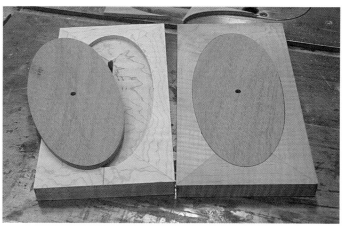

26 Using the same pattern mounted on the inlay wood and the inlay kit bushing, once again run around the pattern to create a matching fit.

27 Slice the inlay to the correct thickness on the table saw and glue into the drawer-front frame.

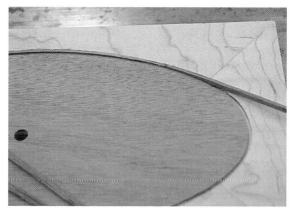

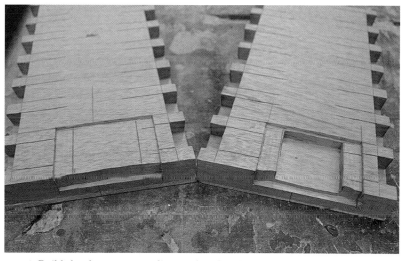

28 Remount the pattern onto the dried, assembled drawer front and using the same inlay kit setup, create a groove around the outside of the pattern. Cut the thin pieces of walnut inlay, apply a bit of glue into the groove and gently coax the pieces into place.

29 Build the drawers according to the plan, but do not assemble the boxes yet. (See "Drawer Basics: Hand-cut Dovetails" on page 8.) Also do the necessary work for the installation of the drawer locks at this time.

30 After you have completed the joinery on the drawers, start the inlay on the top drawers. Set the blade depth to $\frac{1}{8}$" and the fence to $\frac{7}{8}$" and run all four edges against the fence, creating the necessary grooves. Cut matching pieces of walnut inlay and glue into the grooves.

31 Set the blade height to $\frac{7}{8}$" (or just to the edge of the inlay) and remove a $\frac{1}{8}$" piece of material, leaving the walnut strip. Cut the top drawer banding to length, miter the corners and glue into position.

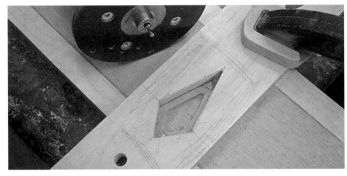

33 Using the inlay kit again, locate and rout the diamond-shaped escutcheons. Place the pattern so that the keys work on the bottle drawer locks. Cut matching inlays from walnut, glue into place, and cut out for the key area. Finish the drawer boxes but do not install the bottoms.

32 Slice the bottle drawer veneer fronts and glue them onto the completed bottle drawer fronts.

34 This is how the tambour door pieces look when assembled into the door panels. To achieve this look, attach $\frac{1}{8}$" pieces onto the $\frac{1}{2}$" piece of the opposing primary wood. Then rip tambour pieces that are $\frac{1}{2}$" thick by the resulting $\frac{5}{8}$" wide. Leave them a $\frac{1}{2}$" longer than the final size.

35 Arrange the pieces as they are to be glued. Set up as shown, with two 3"-wide strips of canvas temporarily tacked to a work surface. Using waxed paper underneath the canvas prevents the glue from soaking through the canvas. It is important to apply enough glue to attach the tambour pieces but not too much as to glue the pieces to each other. Apply the glue to the canvas, place the tambour pieces, and place a second slightly smaller board on top. Clamp along the length of the tambours, tightly to the fence. Then clamp the pieces flat with the necessary number of clamps.

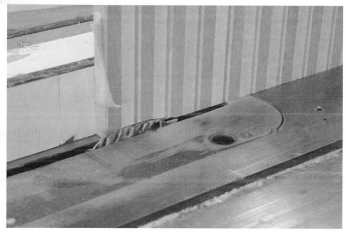

36 With the tambour doors dry, cut to the required length, and form a ¼" rabbet on each end that will ride in the groove in the case. Test the fit on the scrap sample of the corner created earlier. You want a smooth ride (not sloppy) along the track. Wax helps smooth the ride.

37 Cut the tambour pull pieces to size, then inlay the ⅝"-wide opposing wood pieces into the pulls. Create a ¼" × ⅝" rabbet on the back side of each piece as shown, and put an 45°-angle cut on the front side of the rabbeted edge. Mill one of the pulls for the lock.

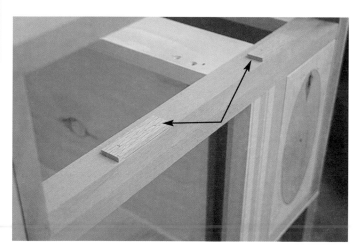

38 Slide in the drawer boxes with the fronts set flush with the case, mark the inside edge of the drawer front, and glue and tack a ³⁄₁₆" block to act as a drawer stop.

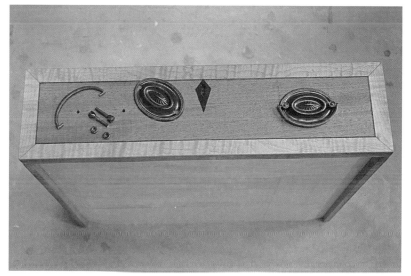

39 Predrill the first slat of each tambour for a No. 6 × ⅞" wood screw. By feeding the tambour doors up from the bottom and into the grooves from where the groove exits the rear, slide the doors to the front. Attach the pulls.

40 Remove the tambour doors before finishing. Final sand all work and apply the finish. I selected oil/varnish finish for this piece to allow the contrasting primary woods to stand apart. (See "Oil/Varnish Finishing" on page 40). To complete the project, install all hardware and set the marble slab in place.

index